CHAPEL

in the

SKY

CHAPEL
in the SKY

KNOX COLLEGE'S

OLD MAIN AND

ITS MASONIC

ARCHITECT

R. LANCE FACTOR

R. Lance Factor

NORTHERN ILLINOIS UNIVERSITY PRESS *DeKalb*

Published by the Northern Illinois University Press, DeKalb, Illinois   60115

Manufactured in the United States using postconsumer-recycled, acid-free paper.

Design by Julia Fauci

Library of Congress Cataloging-in-Publication Data

Factor, R. Lance.

Chapel in the sky: Knox College's Old Main and its

Masonic architect / R. Lance Factor.

p.   cm.

Includes bibliographical references and index.

ISBN 978-0-87580-415-6 (clothbound: alk. paper)

1. Ulricson, Charles, 1816-1887. 2. Old Main (Galesburg, Ill.)–History.

3. Knox College

(Galesburg, Ill.)–History. 4.Freemasonry–United States–History–19th Century.

5. Galesburg,Ill.)–Buildings, structures, etc. I. Title.

LD2815.046 F33 2010

378.773/49 22

To Barbara

Contents

Foreword

For many the daily trip to the office brings the comfort of habit and the expectations of routine. My walks to the office on the third floor of Old Main at Knox College eventually provoked a bundle of questions about the building that could not be deferred. Why do the niches punctuate the corner towers, and why are they so oddly placed? What is the meaning of the crazy-quilt nest of triangles above the east and west doors? Why is the pattern repeated above every door on the interior? Why does Old Main have multi-storied windows, rather than the nearly universal single-story variety?

In the summer of 2006 I found myself on a ladder measuring windows, niches, hooded moldings, foundation stones, mullions, and anything else that could be safely reached before vertigo overwhelmed research. I recorded measurements and calculated ratios, hoping for, and then finding, a long hidden geometric code that defined the features on the exterior. I made my way to the attic of Old Main, where I measured the platform, the bell tower, and the pitch of the roof. I found the missing acanthus leaves that once adorned the Corinthian columns on the bell tower, and I uncovered a section of the original brick wall that retains the cherry red color so prized by the architect and the trustees in 1857.

The life story of Charles Ulricson, the Swedish immigrant architect of Old Main, soon became a part of my detective work. He was an outsider standing by as a general contractor for another firm's designs when the trustees, in frustration over long delays, turned to him and asked for his plans and drawings. To their astonishment, Ulricson quickly submitted a fresh set of plans modeled on the first Collegiate Gothic academic hall in America, the famous New York University, also known as the Chapel in the Sky. Thereafter, the Knox trustees began calling their new architect "The Prompt and Urbane Mr. Ulricson." The Knox solons, nearly all of whom were Anti-Masons, did not know and would have been mortified to learn that the urbane Mr. Ulricson practiced esoteric geometry and maintained close ties with Freemasons. Old Main has an ample fund of embedded symbolism and hidden meanings.

Many visitors to Knox College campus have remarked that the appearance of Old Main is different from the numerous old mains found on other college campuses. Architectural historians treated the building as an unusual example of Collegiate Gothic, finding it stiff and only vaguely Gothic. Prior to the restoration of the exterior in 1933, campus and town observers saw a mixture of styles: Tudor, Norman, Greek, and Gothic. Solving the puzzle of style led to an investigation of how and why the Knox trustees modified the interior and sometimes the exterior in response to the pressing economic and educational issues of the day. The history of a building soon went beyond the record of the man who created it. If the reader gains a renewed appreciation for a famous landmark and for the men and women of Knox College who preserved and continue to preserve a national treasure, I will count my labors as a success. I am grateful for the assistance of Rodney Davis, Matthew Norman, John Norton, Peter Bailley, Marc Safman, Kay Vander Meulen, Ross Vander Meulen, Mary McAndrew, Martin Reichel, Wayne Temple, Jane Davis, Franklin Hartzel, Susan Hall Muelder, Owen Muelder, and the Knox College Faculty Research Fund.

CHAPEL

in the

SKY

A Surprising Irony

Old Main (1857), on the Knox College campus in Galesburg, Illinois, is well known as a national landmark and the only extant building connected to the Lincoln-Douglas debates. Augustana Church (1867) in Andover, Illinois, also known as the Cathedral on the Prairie, is the mother church of the Augustana Synod and a landmark in the Lutheran Church of America. Both are the work of the virtually unknown Swedish-born immigrant architect Charles Ulricson (1816–1887; see fig. 1). Architectural historians cite both landmarks as unusual, even puzzling, examples of the antebellum Gothic Revival style. Eventually Gothic Revival became the "only proper style" for numerous churches and colleges, but the observers who found Ulricson's buildings strangely different are correct. They lack many Gothic characteristics, such as crockets, pinnacles, vergeboards, and other cathedral-like ornaments. Instead they have subtle and unusual features that seem more akin to the Greek Revival style than the Gothic. Knox's Old Main has a highly legible geometry, windows that hint at being columns, a strange design of interlocking triangles and rectangles in its windows, and oddly placed niches that punctuate the corners. Old Main was originally called "Main College." Numerous colleges, especially in the Midwest, had a main college that at some later time became their old main. When Knox's Main College opened on July 7, 1857, many thought that the bell tower looked too much like a Greek temple because it had Corinthian columns supporting Gothic arches. The "pagan" influence seemed too pronounced. It wasn't "Gothic enough." Visitors to Andover—though not the Swedes who had labored for four years to build their cathedral—reported it "unfinished in appearance," and although the new church reminded many of their churches in Sweden, it, too, wasn't Gothic enough. These reactions point to puzzles about architectural style and deeper questions about the meanings of Ulricson's designs: What was his version of Gothic Revival? Where did he learn his craft? What were his aims?

Knox College and Galesburg, Illinois, are fortunate to have three fine histories: two by the late Professor Hermann Muelder, *Fighters for Freedom* (1959) and *Missionaries and Muckrakers* (1984), and another older but still engaging work, *They Broke the Prairie* (1937) by E.E. Calkins. These admirable accounts say little about Charles Ulricson and nothing about his architectural training, nor do they record how or why the Knox trustees hired a Mason in 1855 to build two of their most notable buildings, Old Main and Whiting Hall, the latter of which was then known as the Female Seminary. Augustana Church has never changed its name, but Ulricson's role in creating this great cathedral is similarly obscure. Various histories of Swedish immigration mention Augustana Church as a destination for many hundreds of new arrivals, but only one account mentions Ulricson as " . . . the Swede who had been in America so long he lost his Mother Tongue." [1] Ulricson, who lived and worked in Peoria, Illinois, was an outsider to the Calvinists in Galesburg and the Lutherans in Andover; consequently, he received little more than a mention in college and church histories. Correcting these omissions and oversights reveals a story that sheds light on the formative years of a college, a church, and a town. Ulricson's story provides new information on Midwestern architectural history, and it offers remarkable new interpretations of the antebellum Gothic in Illinois.

Ulricson was a dispossessed aristocrat, a cosmopolitan, an immigrant with ties to both the Swedish and American rites of Freemasonry, and a practitioner of esoteric architecture. His patrons were Anti-Masonic Biblicists who staunchly condemned all secret societies and esoteric philosophy. How an architect who put talismans and mystical symbols in his buildings won permission from his Anti-Masonic patrons to work without scrutiny or supervision and why that outsider risked a career-ending scandal to adorn his masterpieces with secret signs and charms are the animating questions behind the creation of Knox College's Old Main and Augustana Church. Set in the context of a many sided collision of opposing convictions, Ulricson's architecture revolves around a surprising irony, which occurred not once but twice. Anti-Masonic Lutherans hired a Masonic architect to erect their cathedral. And Knox's second president, Jonathan Blanchard, the arch Anti-Mason of the day, hired a Swedish Freemason to build his cherished Main College. Blanchard and the Knox trustees wanted a demure Protestant schoolhouse in "plain style." Ulricson gave them mystical architecture. They sought a restrained exterior; he gave them esoteric geometry. They expected a simple Puritan interior; he supplied the decorations of Freemasonry.

We know little of Ulricson's early work in Peoria. In 1845 he had some connection with Jubilee College as a contractor for an Episcopal bishop, Philander Chase. Bishop Chase drafted his own plans, and although Jubilee is today a reconstructed state historic site, Ulricson's contributions cannot be identified. In 1854 Ulricson built the "fireproof" Hall of Records in Knoxville, Illinois. This technological wonder of the day was a 50 by 30 foot giant iron box with iron shutters, doors, and floors. After it opened, Ulricson quickly gained a regional reputation for making fireproof buildings. Built in the civic Tuscan Revival style, the Hall of Records had two matching wings and a pediment without decoration. It stands today as the Knoxville City Hall. From 1855–1857 Ulricson worked on Knox's Main College and the companion Female Seminary, and in 1867 he directed his fellow Swedes in the construction of their enormous church in Andover, which became the famous Cathedral on the Prairie. For a short time all three structures were the Illinois giants of their day. Augustana Church has a nave 125 feet by 60 feet with seating for a thousand souls. Its tower, which features a steeple ringed with eight slender Corinthian columns, reaches 136 feet. Eight oak beams, each weighing over 5,000 pounds, support a wooden barrel-vaulted ceiling. Augustana's sheer size makes an impression even today. Old Main, Whiting Hall, and Augustana Church each contain more than half a million bricks. After 1867 Ulricson returned to his office in Peoria to begin work on the now lost First Masonic Temple (1870). This four-story behemoth occupied

FIGURE 1—Photograph of Charles Ulricson, date unknown. Special Collections and Archives, Knox College Library, Galesburg, Illinois.

almost half a city block in downtown Peoria. The builder of the small iron box in Knoxville had become known as the master of brick and timber multi-storied fireproof structures. Ulricson's engineering expertise and his versatile skill in Greek, Gothic, and Tuscan styles can be traced to his connections with the New York City firm of Town and Davis, America's leading architects in the pre–Civil War era.

After arriving in New York City in 1835, Ulricson found work, probably as a draftsman, in the studio of Ithiel Town (1784–1844; see fig. 2) and Alexander Jackson Davis (1803–1892; see fig. 3). Davis was America's premier antebellum architect and leader of the Greek, Gothic, Tuscan, and Egyptian revivals. Town was widely regarded as the greatest architectural engineer in America. His patented bridge truss system eliminated the need for stone arches and made the expansion of the railroads possible. His innovative ironwork shop fronts created the modern retail shop, and in the Lyceum of New York (1835–1836), the first natural history museum in America, the celebrated firm of Town and Davis created a multi-storied civic building with a vertical glass wall.[2] Ulricson adapted Town's cast-iron shop fronts for the Hall of Records in Knoxville, Illinois, and he probably used some version of the Town truss to support the upper floors of Old Main. The firm of Town and Davis designed, influenced, or built: the state capitols of Ohio (1839), Indiana (1835), North Carolina (1833), and Connecticut (1827–1831); the Customs House (1833–1840) on Wall Street (now called the Federal Hall National Memorial); the United States Patent Office (1832–1834) in Washington, D.C.; the Pauper's Lunatic Asylum on Blackwell's Island (now called Roosevelt Island) (1834–1837) in New York City; the Wadsworth Atheneum in Hartford, Connecticut (1842–1844); and numerous residences and commercial buildings in New York. Where Town and Davis's designs were not adopted outright, successor architects copied or adapted their designs, as evidenced by the state capitols of Illinois (1837) and Iowa (1840).[3]

Ithiel Town, older partner of Davis and head of the firm, supplied the engineering talent and secured the commissions. Davis handled most of the creative details. Recent scholarship indicates that Town had a deep interest in occult philosophy and esoteric geometry.[4] Town amassed a large library of 25,000 architectural engravings and drawings and more than 11,000 books, which included nearly 5,000 volumes on occult subjects, Neoplatonism, and Freemasonry.[5] Town and Davis were not Freemasons but they did share the Masonic celebration of geometry as an expression of metaphysical and spiritual truth. Town extolled Pythagoras, Euclid, and Newton as seers and conveyers of secret wisdom. He believed that special geometric figures called philosopher's stones communicated with and participated in the mind of the Divine Architect and Geometer of the Universe. These privileged figures had contact with a divine source, and they had the power to reconcile conflicts and divisions. When Davis designed Town's private residence in New Haven, Connecticut, he dedicated almost half the floor space to a library to house Town's enormous collection. Many volumes later went to Yale University and became the nucleus for its library. The dimensions of Town's library and other rooms were set down in lengths of measure known as the Masonic cubit, also called the sacred cubit. As will be shown in later chapters, Ulricson followed this example by repeatedly using the Masonic cubit to establish the dimensions of Knox's Old Main, and, like his mentor, Ulricson crafted window designs that represent the philosopher's stone

Town used his library to search for ancient examples of the geometric philosopher's stone.[6] In medieval alchemy the philosopher's stone was an elixir that could transform chemical elements into their opposites—lead into gold, matter into spirit, and the common into the rare. In esoteric geometry the philosopher's stone is an interlocking set of figures that has the power to preserve unity within conflicting opposites. These elusive figures, along with the special ratios π (pi) and

FIGURE 2—Ithiel Town pointing to "The Book of Mathematical Exercises." Oil portrait of Ithiel Town by Fredrick Spencer. Reproduced with the permission of Center Church-on-the-Green, New Haven, CT.

FIGURE 3—Alexander Jackson Davis. *Sketch of A.J. Davis,* Mary Freeman Goldbeck, circa 1845. Graphite on paper, 14x10 inches. Drawings and Archives, Avery Architectural and Fine Arts Library (1940.00.00740).

Φ (the golden ratio), were thought to transform the building into a talisman suffused with the creative and protective energy of God, the Divine Architect and Geometer of the Universe. The building became a magical charm when imprinted with a philosopher's stone. Architects who used esoteric geometry were practicing an alchemical art. The quest for the geometric philosopher's stone originated in the story that Plato had placed mysterious interlocking figures over the entrance to his academy with the inscriptions "Let None Enter Who Are Ignorant of Geometry!" and "God Ever Geometricizes." Plato's example inspired alchemical architects to position geometric signs in their buildings. It is likely that the complex designs in Old Main's transom windows refer to the entrance to Plato's academy.

The metaphysical themes in the Town and Davis legacy and the presence of philosopher's stones went undetected until the recent discovery of the puzzling brick triangles embedded in a Town building built in 1831 at 211 Pearl Street in New York City. After the horrific destruction of the World Trade Center on September 11, 2001, preservationists conducted a survey of buildings around Ground Zero. At 211 Pearl Street investigators found a brick section of a storefront that was first called the Illuminati Shrine but is now counted by many as one of Town's talismanic signs. The misnamed shrine, which has now been removed and placed in storage to save it from a developer's wrecking ball, is a carefully layered arrangement of interlocking triangles. Another example of a Town and Davis building with a cryptic sign is Federal Hall National Memorial, formerly the United States Customs House. This famous Greek Revival edifice is now the icon of Wall Street and the Financial District. Town and Davis regarded it as one their greatest achievements. Today few visitors would recognize that a golden rectangle is inscribed on the rotunda floor, nor would they surmise that this simple figure surrounded by concentric circles is a piece of esoteric geometry (see fig. 5). John Frazee (1792–1852) designed the interior of Federal Hall following specific suggestions by Town and Davis. Ulricson certainly saw Federal Hall, and from his mentors he learned the deeper reasons for decorating with geometric symbols. Town, Davis, and Ulricson followed the strategy of hiding their strange insignia in plain view. They appear as innocuous geometric decorations, but in all likelihood their purpose was to bring the public into contact with the sacred signs of esoteric geometry. For the architectural alchemist, all who pass under or over a sacred figure received the protection of the Divine Architect. Along with the Town and Davis methods of using iron floors and posts with brick and stone, Ulricson brought alchemical architecture to Galesburg and Andover, where his architecture survives in a remarkably pure form. Ulricson's fireproof Hall of Records has long been known as a local curiosity, but his use of esoteric geometry remained undetected until the summer of 2006 when research for this book revealed his complex and puzzling designs.

FIGURE 4—Federal Hall National Memorial, New York City. Photograph, New York Public Library Digital Library.

FIGURE 5—Federal Hall, detail of rotunda floor with golden rectangle. Photograph, collection of Marc Safman.

Ithiel Town began his study of esoteric geometry by collecting and reading the works and translations of the English classicist Thomas Taylor (1758–1835). Taylor was the first to translate the complete works of Plato, Aristotle, Plotinus, and Proclus into English. To his followers, Taylor's prodigious output opened new worlds of ancient philosophy that offered exhilarating alternatives to both religious orthodoxy and the materialism of the natural sciences. William Blake and William Wordsworth, among many other notable poets and artists, attended Taylor's soirees to discuss the hidden meanings of esoteric philosophy. Ithiel Town may have met Taylor at one of these meetings during his trip to London in 1829. After that trip, Town began amassing his library with books purchased in London. With royalties pouring in from his bridge patent, Town acquired all of Taylor's own writings, including *The Theoretic Arithmetic* and *Introduction to Proclus' Commentary,* along with many of his translations. Taylor's ideas about arithmetic are fanciful restatements and expansions on the Pythagorean idea that physical objects are composed of numbers. With great ingenuity but little mathematical rigor, Taylor purported to show how some numbers have a special relationship to 1. He then argued that the pervasive number 1 represents the ultimate and fundamental One, described by Plotinus as God or Unity. The One creates all things by a process of emanation or outflowing. The effulgence of the godhead establishes a great chain of being, with life and spirit (*Nous*) being the nearest to the One and thus more real. Plants and inanimate bodies, like buildings, are less real because they are further away from the One. Taylor advocated constructing geometric figures with special numbers and ratios that possess what he called "the universal cement."[7] The "cement" is the unity-preserving property of the number 1. Through imaginative sophistical arguments Taylor found ways to relate all sorts of numbers and geometric figures, like pi and the golden rectangle, to the universal cement. If these special figures and ratios were placed in or on inanimate objects, the universal cement moved those objects up the great chain of being. They became more spiritual and more real. It is easy to see that magical thinking influenced Taylor's views on geometry and arithmetic. Taylor attacked algebra as a subject that obscured the presence of the divine emanations. Apparently, he believed that the variables x, y, z hide the sacred numbers. Only arithmetic and geometry could display the beauty and power of unity figures, and according to Neoplatonic teaching, seeing is the purest form of knowing.

Taylor's work had an immediate appeal for Town and Davis. Like others working in the Greek Revival movement, they found the Roman neoclassical style too flexible and unregimented. It followed no rigorous geometric formularies. By contrast, ancient Greek architecture adhered rigorously to strict geometric rules. The Greek Revivalist school believed that those rules constituted the balance, symmetry, and proportion in the beautiful works of the ancient masters, and if Greek Revival was to succeed in America it must have the sacred geometry as taught by Pythagoras, Euclid, and Plato. Like other American followers of Taylor, such as Ralph Waldo Emerson and Bronson Alcott, Ithiel Town organized soirees to read and discuss Taylor's philosophy. He also prepared his own "Mathematical Exercises" to teach his apprentice architects and draftsmen esoteric geometry. Among Town's surviving manuscripts, "The Books of Mathematical Exercises" shows complex figures of interlocking rectangles, triangles, and spirals that unfold and connect in intricate patterns. Town gave special attention to the generative patterns of the Fibonacci series of numbers.[8] These patterns are frequently illustrated today by the examples of the spiral in a sunflower and the partitions in the chambered nautilus. Ulricson, like Town, favored triangles based on the Masonic cubit and the mystical square root of five. In contemporary argot, Town taught his students how to make architectural da Vinci codes. Town valued his pursuit of esoteric geometry and philosopher's stones so highly that he insisted that Frederick Spencer, his portrait painter, show a page of the "Mathematical Exercises," with Town's finger resting on what is thought to be one of his philosopher's stones (see fig. 2). Clearly Town hoped to be remembered for his buildings and his excursions into esoteric geometry. Perhaps his gesture is telling the viewer to look for geometric figures in his buildings. It is likely that Ulricson worked his way through Town's exercise books as part of his training in the great engineer's studio. Learning the practical skills of drafting went hand in hand with lessons in spiritual geometry. Making sacred figures was, of course, a closely guarded guild secret. Town was willing to announce publicly, "I have a strange fascination with esoteric subjects," but he did not explain how his fascination influenced his designs.[9] The general teachings of Neoplatonic philosophy, the doctrine of the great chain of being, and the elevation of geometry as a master science could be openly discussed, as the writings and teachings of Emerson and Alcott make abundantly clear; however, the construction of talismanic figures and the intricacies of Masonic numbers were subjects that had to be treated as carefully guarded trade secrets. Many of Town and Davis's clients and certainly all of Ulricson's clients, except his fellow Freemasons, would have been appalled to learn that Ulricson incorporated elements of esoteric geometry in some of his buildings. The Anti-Masonic hysteria of the 1820s and 1830s multiplied suspicions about all forms of secret societies and arcane knowledge, including the study and practice of esoteric philosophy. The idea that God is the Divine Architect and Geometer of the Universe, though pivotal for alchemists and Freemasons, was an outright heresy for Biblicists and Anti-Masons. For the latter, "The Geometer God" was part of the insidious and heretical deism that had infected the minds of many founding fathers. Men like Benjamin Franklin and George Washington succumbed to the apostasy of deism and joined the fraternity of Freemasons. The Anti-Masonic voices that condemned the compass and squares of the Freemasons would have been equally vehement in denouncing the philosopher's stones of the alchemical architect. Town and Davis realized that it was one thing to discuss philosophy and architecture in their salons and quite another to let the public know the meaning behind their geometric signs.

Today Freemasonry is part of the common cultural history of America, but in Ulricson's day the ancient fraternity repeatedly came under heavy criticism, suspicion, and scrutiny from fundamentalist Protestant leaders, like Knox's second president, Jonathan Blanchard. The Anti-Masonic Party (1828–1838) and its persistent accusations of heresy, conspiracy, and disloyalty eliminated decades of Masonic influence and leadership in civic affairs. Indeed when Ulricson arrived in New York City in 1835, even the oldest colonial lodges that had once welcomed Washington and Lafayette had closed or gone underground. The First Masonic Temple (1824; demolished 1857) was the pride of New York's Freemasons. It appeared in viewbooks along with City Hall and the Merchant's Exchange as one of the three landmarks in the city. The Masonic temple on Broadway was the first stone Gothic building in America. Its unique Grand Hall rested on iron springs to accommodate the dances and celebrations of thirteen participating lodges.[10] As a young man, Davis's engraving of the temple won the attention of New Yorkers and established his ability as a "compositor, " as architectural artists were then called. Town recognized Davis's talent and invited him to become a partner in 1829 (see fig. 6). Ulricson also studied the famous landmark and incorporated its trefoil circular windows and its eight-segment sun windows in Augustana Church. When Masonic membership declined, custodial Grand Masters changed the name of their home to Gothic Hall and rented its central chamber to the Whig Party. The Whig Party, ironically, used the Gothic Hall for Anti-Masonic speeches and rallies. Many churches in antebellum America shared the Anti-Masonic prejudice, and many affirmed the idea that Freemasonry promoted heretical beliefs. In 1866, the General Council of Lutherans in America followed the earlier example of the Calvinist churches and their own long-standing convictions by officially condemning all secret societies as "unchristian."[11] A succession of Lutheran pastors at Andover repeatedly warned their parishioners to avoid secret societies upon pain of excommunication; nonetheless, despite their caution, Anti-Masonic Lutherans called upon Ulricson to build their cathedral, not knowing of his attachments to Freemasonry and esoteric geometry, nor did they know that their Cathedral on the Prairie owed a debt to a Masonic temple.

Jonathan Blanchard and most of the Knox College trustees came of age at the height of the Anti-Masonic campaign. At the founding of Galesburg and Knox College in 1837, the trustees vowed to exclude all secret societies from the campus. Blanchard, as in other matters, went a step further. Ostracism was not sufficient: secret societies must be outlawed and abolished in the town. He went out of his way to expose and excoriate newcomers suspected of being Freemasons, and on one occasion he summarily expelled a student who admitted to being a Freemason. The Reverend Dr. Blanchard had a lifelong antipathy to Freemasonry. He founded and led the second Anti-Masonic party in 1880, accepted its presidential nomination in 1882, and vigorously defended its call for suppression of all secret societies. Arguably Blanchard was the most fervent and persistent enemy of Freemasonry of his time. During his presidential campaign Blanchard claimed that the swelling numbers of Lutherans migrating to America (300,000 by his estimate) would be his allies in the fight against secret societies. In his unpublished autobiography Blanchard wrote, ". . . the Lutherans, who peopled Scandinavia, by the Reformation had given the death-blow to all the Masonic lodges in every portion of Europe."[12] His prediction of a political alliance with the Lutherans proved to be as flawed as his belief that the Reformation had swept the lodges out of Europe. The Lutherans in Galesburg and Andover rejected secret societ-

FIGURE 6—*Masonic Hall,* engraving by A.J. Davis, 1828. Printed by Fenner Sears & Co., NY. Collection of the author.

ies, but they did not make their opinions into a crusade, and few voted for Blanchard in 1882. Moreover, Blanchard did not know that the Swedish Rite of Freemasonry had survived and even prospered under Reformation theology and that some Swedish Americans, like Ulricson, remained attached to the Swedish and American rites.

Blanchard would have been shocked to discover that his Main College was a piece of Masonic architecture. For him, making an edifice to embody the divine architect would be a satanic undertaking, an abomination, a violation of the first commandment against making idols, an act of geomancy, and utterly unacceptable. Still, despite all of his natural caution and his acquired prejudice, in a matter of a few weeks in the fall of 1855 the fulminating President Blanchard cashiered his trusted fellow Calvinists, the Chicago firm of Olmstead and Nickolson, threw out their ostentatious designs, and abruptly hired an outsider. Blanchard and the Knox trustees referred to their new architect as "The Urbane Mr. Ulricson" to acknowledge his aristocratic demeanor. When

FIGURE 7—The Chapel in the Sky. *The University of the City of New York,* 1850, line drawing, New York Public Library Digital Library.

Ulricson quickly produced plans for an academic hall that resembled the famous University of the City of New York, also known as the Chapel in the Sky, the trustees changed their form of reference to "The Prompt and Urbane Mr. Ulricson." They rejoiced in the thought that they would soon have their own Chapel in the Sky. Town, Davis, and their younger partner, James Dakin, designed and built New York University on Washington Park in 1834. It was a stunning four-story white marble hall, the first in America in what Davis called the English Collegiate Gothic style. After Samuel F.B. Morse made it the subject of a landscape painting entitled *The Chapel in the Sky,* admiring New Yorkers gave their new building that name.

The second source for Ulricson's Old Main was the Wadsworth Atheneum in Hartford, Connecticut. The Wadsworth was the mature statement of Town's efforts to incorporate esoteric geometry in the facades of Gothic Revival civic buildings. Previously, Town and Davis limited esoteric geometry to the temple-style buildings in the Greek

FIGURE 8—Wadsworth Atheneum, postcard image taken from a photograph by A.C. Bosselman & Co., NY, circa 1915. Postcard in Special Collections and Archives, Knox College Library, Galesburg, Illinois.

Revival, but as Town neared the end of his career, he invented ways to incorporate sacred geometry in the increasingly popular Gothic Revival style. What had been done for Greek temples, like Federal Hall, must now be done for castles, like the Wadsworth Atheneum. Davis held less enthusiasm for this mission, but he agreed to design the arched entrance of the Atheneum. The shape of the curved arches and the placement of central towers flanking a recessed door have analogs in Knox's Old Main, as do the corner towers and battlements. Ulricson knew that the front of the Wadsworth contained nearly all the formularies for setting windows, moldings, and dimensions in the special ratios of esoteric geometry, and he used his knowledge of these particulars for Old Main.

The Wadsworth Atheneum, the now lost New York University, and Knox's Old Main share many similarities: crenellation, corner battlements, twin parallel towers, matching balanced wings, flanking curved Gothic windows, hooded moldings, and a central curved window called a belvedere window. The deepest connection between the three, however, is not immediately obvious. As shown in later chapters, the hooded moldings and niches in the Wadsworth, Old Main, and Augustana are the keys to unraveling the sacred geometry and its meaning. Old Main's rigorous geometry demonstrates a debt to Ithiel Town, but its central window imitates Davis's work at New York University. Davis's Chapel in the Sky included elegant stone tracery in its chapel windows. Ulricson's elaborate wooden mullions for Old Main's windows recreate the effect of tracery. Moreover, Ulricson adapted Davis's greatest innovation, the elegant window system, known as the (self-named) Daviséan window, a multi-storied vertical window with a decorative panel at floor level. This unique fenestration system is the precursor of the modern vertical strip window in skyscrapers. The Daviséan window can span many stories, and it is quite unlike the more common floor-to-ceiling window that is confined to one story. With remarkable ingenuity Davis used Town's bridge truss to strengthen the floors so that a simple non-load-bearing decorative panel in the multi-storied window could cover the exposed floor joists.[13] Knox's Old Main has a perfectly preserved set of Daviséan windows in a Daviséan Order. A Daviséan Order, again self-named, is a rhythmic and intercolumnar spacing of Daviséan windows that imitates peripteral columns in a repeating pattern on all sides. A peripteral ordering is an evenly spaced row of columns or windows. Knox's Old Main has twenty Daviséan windows in peripteral pattern, and indeed it is the only building in America with an unbroken Daviséan Order. (The evolution of the Daviséan window and why it is regarded as Davis's greatest innovation is found in Chapter 7.) The Daviséan system was rarely copied principally because competing architects didn't know how to do it. Only the firm of Town and Davis and a few of their apprentices understood how to overcome the structural challenge of having floor joists exposed behind a thin decorative panel. The fact that Ulricson understood how to make Daviséan windows provides strong evidence that he had an insider's knowledge of the methods of Town and Davis.

Still, despite many debts to his teachers, Ulricson did not slavishly imitate. On the contrary, he moved in a direction that neither Town nor Davis imagined. In Knox's Old Main and at Augustana Church, Ulricson combined features of two revival styles without falling into a barbarous eclecticism. The Daviséan Order came directly from Greek Revival, as did the carefully worked out symmetry, harmony, and balance of the matching sides. The central curved window, battlements, and parallel towers are unmistakable elements in English Collegiate Gothic. The quoin ashlar blocks at the north and south entrances make a nod to the Egyptian Revival. In each of the three styles he went a step beyond his mentors. Ulricson's applications of esoteric geometry are more extensive and rigorous than Town's version in the Wadsworth Atheneum. Ulricson's windows, being double-hung, are more advanced and more practical than Davis's casement windows. More original still is Ulricson's audacious decision to blend styles. Davis and Town never explored the possibilities of a Greek-Gothic synthesis, but Ulricson did. Moreover, he gave his unique synthesis a distinctive and prominent marker—a bell tower with curved Gothic arches resting on eight Corinthian columns. The Old Main bell tower eventually became the symbol of Knox College, but its initial role was to signal that here was a building that combined Greek and Gothic Revival. Over the decades the bell tower often provoked comment and criticism, but its meaning was lost. On opening day, July 7, 1857, a local newspaper editor said it looked too much like a "pagan temple." In the 1933 campaign to restore Old Main, the chair of the Restoration Committee sent a letter to all alumni reminding them of the unique bell tower and the need for donations to save it. In 1934 the Paramount motion picture *Those Were the Days* prominently featured the bell tower in its movie posters. Their advertisements went a long way to make the bell tower the defining symbol of Knox College, but when the movie crew departed, the college removed the Corinthian columns. Ulricson's most direct reference to an architectural synthesis disappeared.

Successive admirers and caretakers of Old Main knew nothing of Ulricson's goal to make a Greek-Gothic synthesis. He left no record of his intentions, and his natural caution and his knowledge of Blanchard's views kept him from revealing the meanings behind his remarkable designs. Ulricson's belief in esoteric geometry and its power to unify opposites probably gave him the confidence to conceive and execute a Greek-Gothic synthesis as an emblem of the union of reason and faith. Seen one way, the eye discerns the Greek Revival and a clear statement of Attic rationality. Seen another way, the mind contemplates the Gothic and the virtue of piety. When combined, Old Main unites Gothic and Greek, piety and learning, faith and reason. If the columns are restored, the Corinthian-Gothic bell tower will return to its original meaning. Old Main's blend of Daviséan and Townian elements, synthesis of styles, hidden geometry, and cryptic window designs are not found in any other Collegiate Gothic building. Its diverse elements are not flaws in a crude attempt to bring Gothic Revival to the Midwest. Nor is it one among many caught in the tide of campus Gothic. On the contrary, it is one of a kind. This Chapel in the Sky is an exquisite and singular example of alchemical architecture—the finest that stands on American soil.

The Urbane Mr. Ulricson

When Knox's Old Main opened on Monday July 7, 1857, it was known as Main College. This famous national landmark and site of the fifth Lincoln-Douglas debate on October 7, 1858, did not become "old" until 1890, when Knox College built Alumni Hall just thirty yards to the west. In 1857 the Knox trustees celebrated their new Main College and its companion, the Female Seminary (later Whiting Hall) by authorizing the handsome sum of $75.00 for a public dinner.[1] They rejoiced that 1857 saw the completion of Main College, Whiting Hall, a new boardinghouse, and a network of wooden sidewalks to stitch the campus together. The year of great building was almost finished. After spending one fourth of the college's $400,000 endowment for these improvements, the trustees had a campus to match their published claim to be the "third wealthiest college in the nation."[2] Nearly equal amounts of money went to facilities for men and for women, which convincingly demonstrated Knox's commitment to coeducation.

The earliest lithographs and photographs of Old Main show corner battlements, a crenellated center section, and an octagonal platform supporting the bell tower. The battlements, center section, and jaunty finial came down in 1890 when a new hip roof covered the octagon. What the earliest pictures do not reveal are the colors of the building. Old Main and Whiting Hall had cherry red brick as well as windows and doors painted with "two coats of heavy white lead paint."[3] Old Main began its life in an all-American tricolor of red, white, and blue. Ulricson made a special effort to explore Illinois quarries searching for the bluest limestone available. When he found it in Aurora, Illinois, he requested and received extra money from the trustees to purchase thirteen carloads of Aurora Blue Cloud.[4]

The search for Blue Cloud reveals something about the character of Old Main's builder that goes beyond his patriotic motives. Next to his office in Peoria, Ulricson owned and ran a stone yard selling the popular "Athens Marble," a river-bottom limestone found along the Illinois River. Athens Marble was whiter than most limestone, but nothing like true marble. Quarrymen in Joliet, Aurora, and elsewhere invented attractive names to sell their products, and nothing sounds more distinguished and ancient than "Athens Marble." Ulricson could have added to his profits by using stone from his own yard, but he didn't. It mattered greatly that the stone be as blue as possible. On March 24, 1856 Knox purchased 183 perch of Blue Cloud stone for $384 (1 perch = 5 square feet).[5] With 915 square feet of stone for foundations and porches, it is fair to say that Knox's Main College floated on a blue cloud. In May 1856, when Ulricson set the cornerstone and started his red, white, and blue masterpiece, he also became a naturalized American citizen.[6] Ulricson had no idea that just one year after completion, his building would be the stage for the fifth Lincoln-Douglas debate on October 7, 1858, nor could he imagine that his great project would survive to become a national landmark. Ulricson saw his Galesburg projects as milestones in his career. Building the main edifice for a college was a rare assignment in 1857. Completing two multi-storied buildings, a main college, and a female seminary was even more extraordinary. Few architects in Illinois had the chance to shape a college campus in one fell swoop.

Charles Ulricson was born in Stockholm, Sweden, on November 17, 1816 to an upper-class family with ties to the nobility. His father, Karl, held the high government post of "architect to the crown."[7] In his youth Charles had some sort of apprenticeship as a stonecutter and a bricklayer, and he had just started on the family trajectory to join his father's office when his father died suddenly. Shortly thereafter,

FIGURE 9—Old Main, 1864, photograph. Special Collections and Archives, Knox College Library, Galesburg, Illinois.

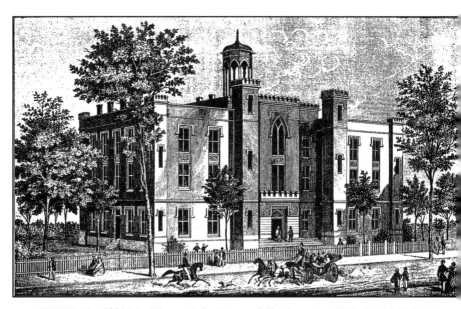

FIGURE 10—*Old Main,* lithograph by Reen and Shoeber, circa 1858. Special Collections and Archives, Knox College Library, Galesburg, Illinois.

Charles and his brother announced a plan to give their inheritance to their mother as soon as Charles reached the age of 21. Although permitted under Swedish law, this transfer aroused the anger of the nobles, and they threatened to keep Charles from entering his father's office. Because the monarchy and the aristocracy controlled access to government positions, Charles and his brother lost all possibility of securing posts in architecture.[8] Indeed, they had little chance of a career at all. That the nobility took an interest in the disposition of the Ulricson inheritance strongly supports the opinion that the Ulrick family moved within elite social circles. The estate of a commoner or a middle-class bureaucrat would be of no interest to the nobles, and they would not have imposed restraints on two young men in a low station. Ulricson's daughter, Frances, believed that her family had some connection with the monarchy and that her grandmother was part of an illegitimate branch of the royal house. If true, this connection accounts for the keen interest of the nobility in the affairs of the Ulricson family. Without independent wealth, Charles's mother could not advance her claims or protect her social position. A normal pattern of inheritance with Charles taking his place as head of the family would bury forever his mother's unrecognized dower rights and her ancestral claims. Charles did not change his mind, and his determination strongly suggests that he was deeply committed to protecting his mother's financial interests and her social standing. Given that he could have conformed to the wishes of the nobility by accepting the inheritance and supporting his mother from his own pocket, it is almost certain that his decision to give real property to his mother indicates that the inheritance issue went beyond matters of finance. Because the nobility interfered in a private matter and continued to pressure the Ulricson family over several years, there are good reasons to believe the claim to aristocratic or royal bloodlines. Frances Ulricson supported her belief in a royal connection with stories of how the royal family entertained her American "cousins" when they made a grand tour of their ancestral country. Such an honor would not go to ordinary visitors, and their reception in the royal palace provided a token recognition of common ancestry.

Fascination with the fiction of the "Holy Grail" as the supposed bloodline of Jesus of Nazareth and Mary Magdalene adds a mythical twist to the Ulricson story. Prior to the ascension of Marshal Bernadotte in 1818 as King Karl XIV Johan, the Swedish monarchs maintained that they were descended from the dukes of Burgundy, who in turn claimed a bloodline going back to the Merovingian kings. The Merovingian line, as legend goes, had its beginning when the son of Jesus and Mary Magdalene became their first king. The Holy Grail in this legend refers not to the cup or dish passed at the Last Supper but instead to the secret of Jesus' offspring and the hidden bloodline. Rolling all these speculations about origins into one giant leap of imaginary pedigree creates a startling new piece of college lore. If Ulricson had the royal bloodline of the dukes of Burgundy and the Merovingian kings, then it follows that a descendant of Jesus of Nazareth crafted Knox College's Old Main. Someone should inform the Knox alumni office.

On a more serious and germane point, the fact that Charles's father had a close connection with the nobility strongly indicates that both father and son were Swedish Freemasons. In early nineteenth-century Sweden, social advancement in the civil bureaucracy, especially in the offices with royal patronage, often depended on membership in the Freemasons. The Ulricson family held a position in a social network that used Freemasonry to promote and protect its interests. Charles's father had compelling reasons to bring his sons into Freemasonry at an early age, and in the Swedish Rite he could do just that. The Swedish Rite is unlike any other branch of Freemasonry in several respects: the king is the hereditary Grand Master (only the present monarch has declined that office, taking instead the title of "Protector of the Freemasons"); the rite is heavily laced with Gnostic and Rosicrucian number mysticism and with the lore of the Knights Templar (so much so that members today make apologies for it); every member must profess a belief in Christianity (other rites require only a belief in God, as a condition for taking oaths); and sons of Freemasons may be inducted in the early degrees as boys (other rites require initiates to be in their majority).[9] There are twelve degrees overall, and the fifth degree gives the initiate rank in the civil nobility. The Swedish Rite provided an avenue for upper-class men to achieve status and patronage.

It is likely that Charles became a Freemason at the age of 12 or 13—sometime after becoming an apprentice in his father's office and after his confirmation in the Church of Sweden. This would have been the first step in assuming his father's mantle and, indeed, a necessary one in order to gain entry into the social network of the privileged classes. His allegiance to Freemasonry continued in America and flourished in Peoria, Illinois, where he kept an office either next to or in the same building as Temple Lodge No. 46. Many years later Ulricson's Masonic affiliation brought him a major commission. In 1870 Charles Ulricson designed and built the First Masonic Temple in Peoria. In the supersecret atmosphere of the day, only a Masonic architect would be entrusted with the task of creating a temple. Shortly after the Masonic temple opened, the Panic of 1873 swept across America. Ulricson lost over $70,000 and fell into ruin when his creditors, some connected to the Masonic temple project, defaulted on their obligations. His debtors simply couldn't or wouldn't pay him, and he had no resources to attach liens. Ulricson never fully recovered from the financial disaster of 1873. Although he received an award at the Centennial Exposition of 1876 in Philadelphia, Ulricson spent his final decade in financial hardship. His strangely worded obituary in December 1887 notes that he was an "Old Settler" but says nothing about his success as an architect, except to note that he built "many buildings."

Charles Ulricson and his brother left Sweden in 1835 bound for two very different destinations. His brother died on the passage to Australia around the time that Charles arrived in New York City with "19 cents in his pocket."[10] There were few Swedes in New York and few in America at the time. From 1835 to 1840, Swedish immigration to America was a mere trickle, with an average of only 67 persons per year arriving in New York City. The great Swedish influx and the opening of the famous Bethel Ship, permanently anchored in New York harbor as a welcome station, came in 1846—almost a decade after Ulricson had arrived. Like Jenny Lind, the famous Swedish Nightingale, and Erik Jansson, founder of the utopian community at Bishop Hill, Illinois, Ulricson's name does not appear on any known passenger lists.[11] Swedish law at this time required a passport fee. Many émigrés had no desire to forfeit money simply to leave a country they would never see again. The money could be better spent on purchasing a passage to America. It is, therefore, likely that Ulricson left Sweden without official permission and traveled under an assumed name. He arrived impoverished, but Manhattan held prospects for a young man with experience in stonecutting, bricklaying, and drafting.

New York had just begun to recover from the disastrous fire of 1835, which had destroyed the oldest parts of the city west of Broadway. Reconstruction began immediately and continued despite the runaway inflation caused by the Panic of 1837. New York's position as the gateway to the Erie Canal and the West kept building activity going at a steady pace; however, much of the new construction was as shoddy as it was hasty. Phillip Hone, one of the founders of the Whig Party and the nearly omnipresent observer of his native New York, recorded in his diary that the building craze went forward recklessly. "Everything [prices] rises in New York . . . nothing falls but the new houses. It is disgraceful to our architects that such things should happen, but it is more the fault of the proprietors; they cannot afford the time necessary to give the building proper stability. The *go–ahead* principle will not do for five-story edifices."[12]

Frances Ulricson reported that her father worked for an architectural firm in New York City.[13] There was only one in 1835–1840. The architectural historian Talbot Hamlin characterized New York construction trade of the 1830s as "chaotic but violently alive . . . with a small reservoir of architectural talent."[14] A young but soon-to-be-famous architect, James Gallier, observed, "On my arrival in New York on the 14th of April, 1832 there was, at that time, properly speaking, only one architect's office in New York, kept by Town and Davis."[15] A second small office didn't open until 1838 when a young Fredric Diaper began his career.[16] Given Ulricson's intimate knowledge of Town's esoteric geometry and Davis's complex multi-storied windows, it is nearly certain that the firm of Town and Davis hired Ulricson, probably as a draftsman. As an employee Ulricson had access to the firm's library of plans and drawings. Both Town and Davis opened their extensive collections of architectural books, models, plans, and drawings to the public as well as to their apprentices. They periodically staged exhibitions of their models in public galleries and they loaned books and plans to interested office visitors who requested them. Both men believed that the public could be educated in "good taste" and that fine architecture could raise the moral as well as the aesthetic standards of the booming metropolis. In 1840 Davis went even further in his mission to educate the public when he ran a series of advertisements inviting visitors to his library to copy his plans and specifications. He made a grand and incredible invitation:

> Amateurs of the Arts, Proprietors of Real Estate about to build, Artists, Professionals, Lecturers, Public press and all persons engaging in Education, *Empirics* by no means excepted, are informed that some thousands of Designs, Books, Paintings, Prints and Specifications for every species of structure in the Assyrian, Egyptian, Greek, Roman, Gothic, Chinese,

Saracen, Moorish, Mexican, and other tastes and styles, *may be seen, com-pared, copied and taken away, free of expense, or questions* (the books and papers being handled with extreme care, and replaced as found at the Library and Office of Alex. J. Davis Architect in the New York University. [Emphasis added].[17]

An empiric is a self-taught man or woman who learns by experience or observation. The term applies to Ulricson's years in New York City. One can imagine the young Swede inspecting Town and Davis's build-ings and plumbing the treasure trove that Davis willingly opened to everyone. It is probable that the ambitious young Swede took advan-tage of Davis's generosity by filling his portfolio with all that could be "compared, copied, and taken away." Ulricson's portfolio gave him credentials that no competitor could match, and it impressed Presi-dent Blanchard and the Knox trustees, convincing them to accept the new English Collegiate Gothic style. By 1842 Ulricson had acquired his American education in the tastes and preferences of his adopted coun-try. He had mastered the popular Greek, Gothic, and Tuscan revivals that would eventually be the foundation of his work in Illinois. He headed South, probably sailing to New Orleans, looking for a place to open his own office, and eventually made his way up the Missis-sippi and Illinois rivers to the rapidly expanding city of Peoria, Illinois. During his first decade in Peoria, from 1844–1854, Ulricson earned a solid reputation for quality construction. As a founding member, in 1847, of the newly formed St. Paul's Episcopal Church, Ulricson built their first small brick church in 1849. In 1854 the county board of Knoxville, Illinois, selected his design for the "fireproof" Hall of Records. His unique building, which is today City Hall of Knoxville, Illinois, has 1,500 square feet with extra thick brick walls, iron case-ment shutters covering all the windows, and an iron floor and ceiling. The Hall of Records is virtually a giant iron box with airtight shut-ters to seal and protect its contents. The novelty and the success of this fireproof box won the attention of President Blanchard. Fire was the great destroyer of brick and timber, and architects employed all sorts of schemes and strategies to defeat the threat of fire. Ithiel Town worked on the problem and developed the techniques for making iron storefronts in commercial and public buildings. Heavy traffic on the first floor, the use of candles and lanterns, and the prevalence of open fireplaces and coal stoves made these buildings vulnerable to careless acts that caused fires. Town and Davis attempted to solve the problem by using stone and iron on the first floor and putting mortar between floor joists on the upper floors. Ulricson followed suit by giving the center section of Old Main an iron floor and numerous iron posts on the first floor to support the upper two floors. Both floors had mortar between the joists.

During work on the Hall of Records, Ulricson established a connection with the growing Swedish population in Knoxville and Galesburg. He hired many Swedes as his day laborers and subcontractors. He met Pastor Tufve Hasselquist (1816–1891), the Lutheran pastor of Swedish-speaking congregations in Knoxville and Galesburg. In 1863 Haselquist became president of Augustana College in Rock Island, Illinois, and he, in turn, recommended Ulricson to the congregation in Andover, Illinois, when they began planning their great cathedral in 1865. In 1855 Galesburg alone had more than 4,000 Swedes out of a population of nearly 10,000.[18] These new citizens along with Irish immigrants provided the labor for the booming town and its rapidly expanding railroads. Ulricson's reputation among the Swedes of western Illinois grew rapidly, especially after he employed scores of his countrymen in the construction of Whiting Hall and Old Main. Work on both began early in 1856. President Blanchard understood that Ulricson's connections with the Swedish labor force were crucial for bringing Whiting and Old Main to the rapid completion he so earnestly sought. President Blanchard wanted close relations with the Swedish community. He saw Swedes as future allies in his war against secret societies. Having Ulricson work for Knox College, first as a superintendent and later as architect, cemented relations with a group that Blanchard treated as his allies. Ulricson's ability to command and to control his workers is evident in an incident reported by his son, Oscar. During the construction of Old Main, a thief "touched Ulricson for the payroll on the train from Peoria."[19] After that incident, to protect his person and his purse, Ulricson distributed the payroll on an irregular basis without prior notification to the workmen. This caused a hardship for the subcontractors and the workers because they could not know on what day or even what week they would be paid; however, despite this inconvenience, no one protested this policy.

In addition to his demonstrable skills in design and drawing, Ulricson had the kind of social bearing that impressed the Yankee elites of Galesburg. President Blanchard and the Knox trustees frequently

referred to him in print and in speech as "The Urbane Mr. Ulricson"—
and with good reason. Ulricson was quite unlike the other Swedes
pouring into Galesburg after the breakup of the utopian community
at Bishop Hill. His upbringing in an upper-class family, familiarity
with aristocratic etiquette, and his experiences in New York gave him
a demeanor that quietly attracted notice and instilled trust. Ulricson
was cultured, literate, reserved, and reliable. His sophisticated man-
ners, composure, and reserve—all so evident in his portrait—reflected
the norms of a high-status family in Stockholm. His decision to leave
Sweden and his perseverance in learning American architecture reveal
a man of courage, intelligence, and resolve. He needed all of these
qualities to persuade the Knox trustees to accept his version of the
Gothic Main College.

Ulricson's temperament and character are revealed in the record
of his actions as a lifelong member of St. Paul's Episcopal Church in
Peoria.[20] There were no Lutheran churches in Peoria when he arrived.
Like many Swedes in America before the great influx of the 1840s,
Ulricson joined the Episcopal Church. In church politics, Ulricson
was an unswerving conservative. He believed in ritual, hierarchy,
and tradition. In the decades before the Civil War, his High Church
commitments put him in a minority. In the formative years St. Paul's,
like other frontier congregations, operated on democratic and egalitarian principles of decision making with little contact or control from
clergy and bishops. St Paul's was openly evangelical and eager for new
members. The congregation decided most matters by a vote—often
with women in full participation—and almost entirely without clerical supervision. Clergy made occasional visits while traveling a circuit.
Episcopal congregations sought ecclesiastical recognition, as a matter
of identity, but resisted oversight and control. In Peoria the first group
of Episcopalians to form a congregation took the name St Jude's. They
maintained their independence so resolutely that Bishop Philander
Chase at nearby Jubilee College in Brimfield, Illinois, simply ignored
them. Bishop Chase, the founder and builder of Kenyon College in
Ohio, usually had his way, and if he didn't establish authority immediately, he waited for the self-organizing congregation to come to
him. After St. Jude's dissolved, possibly from lack of diocesan support,
Bishop Chase tentatively recognized a successor congregation in the
group that called themselves St. Paul's Church. Its members did not
immediately acknowledge his authority and leadership. Accordingly,

the bishop's attitude was one of suspicion, and his support extended no further than the shipment of hymnals. In 1845 Ulricson pushed for greater contact and supervision from Bishop Chase, and eventually Ulricson worked for Chase in some capacity during the construction of Jubilee College. Gradually the fledgling St. Paul's warmed to the prospect of being taught and led by the imposing bishop, who was a very large man in girth, stature, and voice. Ulricson and others in the congregation recognized Bishop Chase's authority and invited the bishop's supervision. The Episcopal hierarchy slowly brought St. Paul's under its control by repeatedly sending conservative clergy. Each priest created a new round of friction between the democratically inclined Low Church families and the High Church loyalists.

Prior to and during the Civil War, St. Paul's rector, the Rev. J.M. Wait, openly defended the institution of slavery. In response to the Emancipation Proclamation, Rev. Wait preached a sermon denouncing President Lincoln's authority to abolish slavery in the rebellious states. His basis for the claim flowed from the standard rhetoric of divine justification for slavery that was voiced all too often by the antebellum Episcopal Church. It didn't sit well with the men and women of St. Paul's in 1863. With sons, brothers, and fathers fighting for the North, the congregation immediately shunned Rev. Wait and his family. Whatever Rev. Wait lacked in wisdom, he certainly made up for in foolhardy pronouncements, for rather than retreat in the face of nearly universal disapproval, he compounded his offenses by declaring that he was a Democrat and that all who listened should support the peacemaking propos- als within the Democratic Party in the election of 1864. Many in the congregation soon accused him of being a traitor and a Cop- perhead. The congregation increasingly shunned and ignored Rev. Wait and his family, with the exception of Charles Ulricson and his young bride, Maria Cowan Ulricson. When the Rev. Wait left town for an extended trip on church business, Maria and Charles went to see how Mrs. Wait and her young family fared. The door was locked and no one answered the door. Ulricson struck a hard blow on the door. The children inside cried and called out for help. When the Ulricsons forced the door open, they found the children weeping and desperately hungry. Mrs. Wait had fallen ill and taken to her bed after locking the children in the house. All were grateful for the food and kindness that the Ulricsons distributed.[21]

Rev. Wait returned with another unpopular idea, auricular confession, or the confessing of sins to a priest. This practice divided the congregation, and many refused Wait's recommendation, but again the Ulricsons dutifully supported their rector. Still, by the end of the Civil War, Rev. Wait had become so unpopular that he was forced to leave. His successor, the Rev. W.H. Roberts, also favored conservative ideas. He wanted the church to have an elevated altar. Without informing the vestry or congregation of his plan, Roberts convinced Ulricson to build a three-stepped altar during one long session of construction on a Saturday night. Working through the night, Ulricson constructed the platform with the required three steps leading to the altar. He then covered the altar with a bright red altar cloth, which he had purchased and saved for the occasion. As dawn broke, Ulricson and Rev. Roberts waited for morning service. When the doors opened, the congregation entered and gasped in surprise and shock. There was an immediate uproar, and a heated argument began. Accusations of deception, betrayal, and high-handedness flew at Ulricson and Roberts. Powerful Low Church families, like the Tyngs and the Kelloggs, refused to leave until the platform and steps came down. The High Church families held their ground and shouted back, demanding proper observance and respect for priestly authority. Angry words flew back and forth, exposing the deep division between the partisans of congregational democracy and those for hierarchical authority. The row continued until finally Ulricson and Tyng inched toward a compromise: they agreed to remove one altar step, and the red altar cloth was taken away and returned to Mr. Ulricson with the agreement that Mr. Tyng would supply a green altar cloth.[22]

During the construction of Augustana Church a decade later, Ulricson had a similar confrontation with the Low Church members of that congregation. The building committee told Ulricson exactly what they wanted for the dimensions and decorations of their church. For the central ornament on top of the towering steeple, they choose a cross attached to a sphere. Ulricson proposed an urn. He argued that the urn is "an empty sign" or "a sign that said nothing."[23] The meaning of symbols mattered to Pastor Swensson and his congregation. They argued among themselves about the propriety of an urn as opposed to the cross and globe. Few outside of Freemasonry knew that the urn often appeared on the exterior of Masonic lodges as a rooftop decoration.[24] The isolated congregation in western Illinois did know that the urn represented mortality. It was not an empty symbol, as their architect had told them.

They rejected Ulricson's explanation and his proposal, but what should take its place? A small faction loudly protested that a cross would indicate that their church was Roman Catholic; others found it acceptable as a reminder of churches in Sweden. The controversy simmered and occasionally erupted into heated debate. Pastor Swensson insisted on "a beautiful gold gilded cross." The malcontents smoldered and carped as the steeple went up, and when they arrived one day to see the globe and cross in place, a howl of protest rained on the pastor and the architect. Ulricson simply ignored all complaints about the cross, but Pastor Swensson was vexed beyond reason. The dissenters gave him no peace. He wanted the cross, but he also wanted harmony in his congregation. Because the congregation was building the church, they had to cooperate to complete the project. A complex system of work exchange guided construction. While one group of farmers laid brick, another grouped worked their farms. After a time the duties were reversed. If this system of mutual support failed, construction would stop, and thus "for the sake of peace," as the pastor said to his congregation, the cross must be removed; however, Ulricson and the elders on the building committee refused to take it down. Ulricson wrote to Pastor Swensson, "If those few who now oppose the symbol of our faith adorning the summit of God's holy temple, and they do not believe in that symbol, they are, as I intimated, but hypocrites, safer out of the Church than in it, and God will make them powerless, their threats will be naught, and shame will be their reward."[25] At a height of 132 feet, it was no easy matter to remove the cross. Gradually the dissenters relented. The cross remains today. Ulricson could be tactful and diplomatic but also decisive and resolute. As the project at Andover expanded, the congregation of yeomen farmers made plans to mortgage their farms to pay for materials they could not manufacture themselves. When Ulricson learned of the mortgage schemes, he wrote Pastor Swensson an urgent letter advising against all mortgages. Work could proceed as funds became available, and the church could be finished in due course without debt.

These vignettes of church life reveal that Ulricson loved ceremony, tradition, hierarchy, and clerical authority. In maintaining these preferences he probably found something closer to the church and the Masonic lodge of his youth. This early period of his career reveals a man who worked from conviction, held an unpopular position, gave prudent advice, showed compassion, and, when necessary, worked in secrecy.

3

Freemasons and Anti-Masons

When Main College opened on July 7, 1857 there were no trees, no paved streets, and no county courthouse in College Park. Nothing stood between Old Main and Whiting Hall. Open fields formed a perfect space for a crackling good party, and the town of Galesburg took advantage of an open campus by hosting a Fourth of July celebration complete with speeches, music, and fireworks. As darkness descended, the magistrates lit bonfires, a band played stirring marches, and the locals set off their firecrackers, phosphorous bombs, and turpentine flares. In the smoky glow of the night sky the red, white, and blue of Knox's new buildings captivated nearly everyone. The next day the *Galesburg Free Democrat* declared the celebration a success. Firecrackers and flares had injured two boys, but there was only one fight with slingshots between "the Swedes and the Irish." These incidents didn't change the general opinion that this Independence Day surpassed all others in marking the prosperity of the town and gown.[1] As heirs of the Puritan church, the Knox trustees didn't believe in ceremony, ritual, pomp, or vanities. They were proud of the fact that Knox College gave no honorary degrees and had no valedictory. They did not celebrate Christmas, and to prove immunity from medieval festivals the trustees made a point of holding a working meeting on Christmas Day every year. To celebrate their new Main College, they hosted a public dinner at a cost of $75.00 on July 7, but everyone knew that the real celebration was held on the Fourth of July. On that day everyone saw two new academic buildings nearly finished and ready to welcome students. Ulricson didn't finish Main College until the middle of August 1857, and students didn't enter the building until September. Still, the appearance of the public square and the adjoining park had changed dramatically. Two tall buildings defined the north and south boundaries of the park, and both overlooked the center of the bustling railroad town.

With a public dinner that coincided with fireworks and patriotic cheer, the trustees hoped to deflect attention from their own bickering and dissension. All their messy infighting had been exposed to the public when on the morning of commencement, June 25, 1857, a group of men and women students gathered on the north porch of the unopened Main College to protest the firing of President Blanchard.[2] The students cheered for President Blanchard, made speeches denouncing George Washington Gale, and signed resolutions calling on the board of trustees to keep Blanchard in office. Soon nearly all of the senior class joined the protestors, announcing that they would boycott their own commencement scheduled for later that afternoon. The seniors called their protest a "self-dismissal." Only one senior, the son of a Knox trustee, took his degree. Thus, the first commencement in the shadow of the new Main College saw only one graduate.[3]

The commencement of one marked the culmination of years of contentious wrangling between George Washington Gale, founder of the town and Knox College, and Jonathan Blanchard, Knox's crusading and fulminating second president. Despite their similar backgrounds and theologies, the two leaders and their factions contested nearly every aspect of college and community life. Church polity: Was Knox College Presbyterian or Congregational? Abolition: immediate or gradual? Slaveholders: punishment or leniency? Sabbath observance: strict or flexible? Temperance: total or partial? Ban on fraternities: absolute or provisional? Building program: accelerated or deliberate? And so on. The two titans and their followers did agree on the importance of coeducation centered on Protestant values. They had no disputes about spending money for both the Female Seminary and Main College. Everyone favored that. They agreed on the need for a modern curriculum that included natural science as well as classics, philosophy, and rhetoric. The entire west side of Main College on the first floor had a chemical laboratory with up-to-date equipment. The third floor had a library as large as the laboratory, and the entire center section of the third floor housed a rhetorical room for the much-anticipated debates between the two literary societies, Adelphi and Gnothautii. As if to hold the center between science and rhetoric, the second floor housed a philosophical lecture hall, the president's office, and a chapel. Ulricson's floor plan depicted a harmonious vision of the liberal arts with natural science, humane letters, and religion peacefully coexisting under one roof.

The reality of the war of the titans and the drama of a student revolt stood in sharp contrast to the expectation that Main College would exemplify a common religious purpose and a shared vision of Protestant education. Many hoped that opening day would sweep aside the controversial firing, the student revolt, and the embarrassing commencement of one. That did not happen. In response to a howl of protests from alumni and students, the two warring factions eventually reached an awkward compromise. Gale would resign his position on the faculty. Blanchard would stay on the faculty for one additional year. The trustees invited the self-dismissed students to return and then postponed opening day for the fall session of 1857 by one week to allow invitations to circulate. The new school year would begin with a grand reception in the resplendent chapel. "The College Students, Male and Female, including preparatory classes, will now meet the College Faculty in the College Chapel in the (new) main Building on Thursday next week [Sept. 2, 1857] at half past 8 o'clock A.M."[4] The attraction of returning to a glorious new building at a college that had made good on its promise to be counted among the best institutions in the country proved irresistible to many. This announcement indicates that although women had their own chapel and classrooms in the Female Seminary, both sexes attended chapel in Old Main. Increasingly Main College became less and less of a male preserve, and by 1862 women were taking classes with men in Old Main. In the fall of 1857 Knox students returned to enjoy in spectacular completion what had been, just months earlier, a churning construction site. At a time when classrooms in Knox's older buildings, East and West Bricks, were small stuffy boxes, the classrooms in Main College, by comparison, were palatial. When Main College opened, students and townsfolk marveled at its large rooms and grand staircase. The view from the top of the central window offered a breathtaking perspective on the thriving town. The chapel alone was a wonder. At 34 feet wide and 67 feet in length and with a height of 29 feet, it occupied the entire second and third stories on the east side. Light from five multi-storied windows filled the room and illuminated the highly varnished oak ceiling and its trefoil designs. Rows of benches accommodated one hundred people and equaled the seating capacity of Galesburg's largest churches. In Illinois few structures offered a comparable atmosphere of space and light. Indeed, in 1857 only the Illinois State Capitol exceeded Knox's Main College in size and mass.

Although unintended, the success of Ulricson's design went a long way toward healing the pain of the Gale-Blanchard war. For Knox students the convocation of 1857 in the new chapel signaled the end of the Blanchard years and marked the beginning of a time when Old Main itself and not individual presidents and personalities gained the loyalty of Knox College alumni. Old Main's perfect symmetry and its four entrances at each of the compass points made it a welcoming edifice. Students could quickly enter and exit. The only point of restriction was the stairs, but even here there were few delays. When the bell tolled, students moved quickly from one class to another. To the discerning eye of a Freemason, the Knox chapel resembled a lodge hall. Freemasons preferred a meeting room on a second floor or higher—in order to be away from prying eyes—and they traditionally sat on a platform on the south side of a room. In the Knox chapel the Knox faculty, called tutors, sat on the south side on an elevated platform. The students sat facing the east wall, where a single lectern formed the focal point of the room. In the lodge, the Grand Master stood in this location. Ten-feet wide folding doors with elaborate Gothic panels gave the doorman control of the only entrance, much like the Tyler of a lodge.[5]

Ulricson's connections to Freemasonry situated him in a social organization quite unlike those of his Congregational and Presbyterian clients. Freemasonry in the mid-nineteenth century was more than an organization with secrets (as it is today). It was a secret organization that acted as a mutual aid society. Brothers helped brothers. The pattern of hatching hidden stratagems to benefit one's own kin is as ancient as any human artifice could be, but Freemasonry wrapped mutual aid in the double cloak of ritual and secrecy that transcended the requirements of kinship and ethnic identity. Freemasonry's ethic of universal brotherhood allowed isolated and dispossessed newcomers, along with well-established middle-class men, to join together in a fraternity that promoted their mutual interests. Ulricson had a natural affinity for this kind of social pattern because it emulated the way the elites in Sweden preserved their class interests. His Masonic network could replace the class system that had excluded him. At the same time the attraction of the egalitarian structure in American Freemasonry mattered to an ambitious immigrant. The lodges practiced democracy by ignoring all differences among those who were admitted. Each member could progress and execute the various high offices. Ironically the lodges practiced democracy with the pomp and circumstance of a hierarchy. The office of Grand Master stood at the top, and the apprentices were at the bottom; however, over time the initiates ascended the hierarchy, with each man taking a turn at the higher offices. Freemasonry excluded many, including free blacks and women, and its secrecy and selective membership set it apart from democratic organizations, like political parties, but within the walls of the lodge an immigrant could experience equality with others without regard to social origin or status. American Freemasons, unlike their Swedish counterparts, did not exact heavy penalties on errant members. The Swedish Rite combined membership with patronage; American Freemasonry combined membership with mutual assistance.

In America Ulricson had the benefits of a fraternity free from the control and discrimination of the nobility. American Freemasonry and its countless derivative groups from Odd Fellows to the Knights of Columbus prepared the immigrant for the struggles imposed by an alien culture. Lodges and fraternities espoused individual self-reliance while inwardly forming hierarchically ordered groups that aimed at mutual assistance. Democracy and hierarchy are opposing social structures, but not in the lodge. The hierarchy was fluid and tied to ritual; the social interaction was egalitarian and tied to fellowship and aid. This paradox makes sense in a culture that was both individualistic and practical. The democracy and doctrine of the lodge protected and nurtured individualism; the mutual assistance of the fraternity made the problems of life easier to solve. Freemasonry espoused the example of "The Ideal Artisan."[6] A man shapes his own destiny by improving his moral character, by living a life of service, and by following the rituals of Freemasonry. The artisan metaphor captured the analogy between making artifacts and making or improving moral character. Freemasonry expressed its ideals in terms of building, crafting, and constructing the habits and sensibilities of honorable men. The profession of architecture had a special place in the lore of Freemasonry because the practicing architect was "The Ideal Artisan" in his profession as well as through his aspirations. The regular Mason could embrace the example of a Solomonic builder in a speculative or spiritual sense. A Freemason identifies with virtues exhibited by the workers and masons who built King Solomon's Temple. For the working architect the symbolic identity of being one of Solomon's builders carried actual as well as ritualistic responsibilities. Being a Masonic architect carried the obligation of applying the principles of Masonic doctrine to the real world of stone and mortar.

Freemasons embraced the notion that it was their civic obligation to sanctify a public edifice. Americans are accustomed to thinking of houses of worship as sacred spaces consecrated by a ritual, prayer, and the proper ecclesiastical authority. For some families the same can be said of the practice of "blessing" the home. Today public buildings and schools serve utilitarian ends. They exist in a practical world governed by secular symbols. At best they commence with a tepid ground breaking and a declaration from the mayor or a public dignitary. The iron wall separating church and state keeps secular dedications free from any notion of sanctification; however, in the early days of the American republic up to the time of the Anti-Masonic campaign, and again after the Civil War, Freemasons openly performed their rituals of consecrating public buildings. The Anti-Masonic campaign extinguished the practice in some parts of the country, roughly from 1835 to 1860, but the panoply of setting cornerstones to be "true and level" returned in the Gilded Age with an even greater flare. The ceremony was solemn, symbolically rich, and highly suggestive but not religious in the accepted sense of the term. The cornerstone rituals reminded the public of the example of Solomon's Temple as a building consecrated for and by the Divine Architect of the Universe. At the cornerstone ceremony, no one uttered prayers, read scripture, or referred to the Christian creeds or sacraments. The whole affair was dignified, colorful, and pious while being impressively non-Christian. In giving visible evidence of a pervasive secular morality that competed with Christian teachings, cornerstone ceremonies offended many Biblicists. The parade leading up to the ceremony temporarily broke the bonds of secrecy by allowing Masons to appear in full regalia. Curious crowds felt the power and the allure of the fraternity when they observed, with surprise, the number of men with familiar faces who wore lavish costumes decorated with strange symbols. Sometimes the parades aroused deep suspicions, in part because the meanings of symbols on the aprons were a mystery to non-Masons. The march to the building site gave public witness to the status of Freemasons as civic marshals somehow blessed with the power to sanctify a new city hall or a courthouse. Men marching in full Masonic costume, like a medieval festival on a saint's day, proved that the Divine Architect and Geometer of the Universe had a real and powerful following. This impressed some while alarming others. The cornerstone ceremony itself revealed little about the workings of the lodge or the rituals of Freemasonry. Masons could appear to be indispensable public servants capable of sanctifying buildings without disclosing even a bit of their controversial doctrines to public scrutiny.

The high point of these Masonic inaugurations, which are now replaced with lackluster ribbon cuttings or spades of dirt, occurred on September 18, 1793. On that day President Washington donned full Masonic regalia, including an elaborate apron, and marched down the recently cleared Pennsylvania Avenue to set the cornerstone of the Capitol. Washington was joined by scores of fellow Masons, also in full costume, from the surrounding Virginia and Maryland lodges. They sang songs, waved banners, and beat drums. Washington's action confirmed Masonry's civic mission while giving witness to Washington's widely circulated declarations about the fraternity: ". . . we will receive from our fellow citizens testimonies of approbation for exertions to promote the public welfare. To enlarge the sphere of social happiness is worthy of the benevolent design of a Masonic institution; and it is most fervently to be wished that the conduct of every member of the Fraternity may tend to convince mankind that the great object of Masonry is to promote the happiness of the human race."[7]

Anti-Masons had a difficult time discounting the example of George Washington. They found it easier to attack the cornerstone ceremony than the man. Knox's Main College, of course, had no cornerstone ceremony and no real opening ceremony. Certainly the trustees had no thoughts of calling on the handful of Freemasons in Galesburg to emulate Washington at the Capitol. Still, as the final chapter of this investigation will show, there is strong evidence embedded in the south wall of Old Main that points to Ulricson's strategy of using the sun's position on the summer solstice to create a kind of annual renewal of the sacred geometry. June 21 is St. John's Day, and in the Masonic tradition this day is the proper time to set cornerstones. An alchemical architect who was also a Freemason would have a strong reason to rectify the missing cornerstone ceremony by using the long shadows cast on the summer solstice to define parts of the building. To the good Puritans of Knox, a cornerstone was just the first of many stones in the foundation—nothing more or less. Because Scripture says nothing about setting academic buildings to be "true and level," no good Christian should take notice of a cornerstone ritual. Indeed the earliest Knox catalogs point out that the college had no ceremonies and no honors of any kind. The students echoed this fact in their literary magazines: "Knox College bestows no valedictory, and dispenses neither honors nor prizes. To the Faculty this mode of appeal to the good behavior and diligence of the students has always appeared of questionable propriety."[8] Commencement at Knox featured neither ceremonies, honors, nor prizes. There was a baccalaureate service and prayers at commencement, but those were safely within the prescriptions of Protestant liturgy. It is significant that it was the Knox faculty, not the trustees, who proposed that Abraham Lincoln receive the college's first honorary degree in 1860. This move signaled the end of Blanchard's strict policy of denying awards and honors, and it could only happen after Blanchard had departed for Wheaton College.

President Blanchard was more extreme than others in his belief that Freemasons were heretics. He is best described as a fulminating Anti-Mason. To Blanchard, Freemasonry promoted blasphemy and Satan worship: "Freemasonry and the Bible give opposite answers to the question of salvation, the one . . . promises salvation by ceremonies, which in effect is salvation by Satan; the other by Christ. The great power of the lodge, as of all false religions, is in its worship. The devil is its god, whom the Bible calls a serpent, and he charms men, as literal snakes charm their victims, and then swallows them."[9] Masonic ritual and, by association, its art and architecture produced false idols. To Blanchard, the idea that geometry could somehow sanctify a building by putting pieces of the Divine Architect into a material artifact was "geomancy," a form of necromancy and a violation of the first commandment. In addition, Blanchard believed that Freemasons were disloyal and unpatriotic because they took so-called "higher oaths" that contravened civil oaths and jurisdictions. To Blanchard, Masonic oath taking simultaneously acknowledged demonic powers and gave obedience to foreign nations. In due course he came to believe that Freemasons fomented the Civil War and Confederate soldiers won victories by calling on Union soldiers at the high point of a bayonet charge to give the secret sign of acknowledgment among brothers.

Nearly all of the trustees and most of the founding families of Galesburg emigrated from upper New York State between 1837 and 1842. As young men and women, they grew up in an area that burned with Anti-Masonic fever. The Knox founders knew the platform of the Anti-Masonic Party. They had witnessed and shared in the hysteria that swept along the Erie Canal and Mohawk Valley and exploded in the East and South with a fury that drove men out of the lodges. In New York State in 1825 there were 480 lodges with 20,000 members; in 1832 there were 88 lodges with 3,000 members.[10] In nearby Vermont, Blanchard's home state, all the lodges closed. The success of the Anti-Masonic movement and the sudden collapse of lodges between 1826 and 1836 convinced many Knox affiliates that the hand of divine justice had defeated Freemasonry. What else could explain its rapid decline? In Galesburg, Illinois, the Knox trustees and community leaders determined to keep their new town and college free of what they saw as the insidious evil of Freemasonry.

A good example of Blanchard's early and intense dislike for Free-masons is found in the story of a Knox student named Hiram Gano Ferris.[11] In 1846 Blanchard expelled Ferris for his outspoken defense of Freemasonry and his public admission that he belonged to a lodge. Ferris had to go, but he was no pushover. At the age of twenty-four Ferris was one of the older students enrolled in the fledgling college and certainly one of the toughest. Two years earlier he had been deputy sheriff of Hancock County. There he distinguished himself by arresting the prominent Mormon leader Orrin Porter Rockwell for the murder of Franklyn Worrell. The arrest scene was a classic stare down. Rockwell drew his gun, declaring loudly that he would use it. Ferris immediately drew his pistol and pointed it directly at Rockwell's face. The older man blanched and dropped his arm.[12] Ferris could match Blanchard in a test of wills just as he had matched Rockwell, and he did. He was not intimidated by Blanchard's practice of publicly sham-ing students in chapel or his heated denunciations of Freemasonry. When expelled, Ferris immediately threatened to sue the college. This led Gale and his faction to support reinstatement. Knox College had few students in 1846 and few resources to fight a lawsuit. The wealthy days of a flush endowment came a decade later. Moreover, the trustees, but not Blanchard, recognized that they had a weak case. Ferris would win in the courtroom, and everyone knew that he had the nerve to take the issue there. Reluctantly the trustees reinstated Ferris. Ferris, in turn, took his vindication as a sign to leave Knox and depart for the goldfields of California. He eventually returned to Hancock County with enough gold to open a bank.

The Ferris incident moved Blanchard to redouble his preaching against secret societies in the belief that frequent attacks would keep Freemasons away from his college. He required the college treasurer to enter the word "Mason" in the *Knox Ledger* next to the names of workmen known to be Freemasons.[13] Blanchard preached against all secret societies, and he refused to let Selden Gale, the son of George Washington Gale, use college buildings for meetings of the Sons of Temperance, a secret society of men and women dedicated to prohibition.[14] In his unfinished autobiography Blanchard said that he kept Freemasons out of Galesburg until 1855. In that year George Lanphere, a local druggist, head of the Democratic Party in Galesburg, and friend of Senator Stephen Douglas, held lodge meetings in his store on the public square just a few yards from Blanchard's pulpit in First Church.[15] Blanchard blamed Lanphere for giving Knox students their first taste of "brandy" and for exposing them to the ideas of Freemasonry and secret fraternities. These claims are misleading. As the Ferris incident indicates, the seeds of Masonry and secret fraternities were in the air, ready to land and take root when conditions were right. In 1855 a handful of Knox men secretly formed a chapter of Beta Theta Pi. It went undetected but did not survive the call to arms that took Knox men into the Civil War. College men had access to local spirits made from prairie plants in the form of blackberry wine and gingerroot wine, which they called "champagne." They didn't need to rely on Lanphere when the Swedes who worked on campus offered a ready supply.[16] Still, if Lanphere did offer brandy, it is likely that he extolled the virtues and conviviality of Freemasonry.

Freemasons around Illinois admired Lanphere as one of the leaders of Illinois Masonic Company B. During the Mexican War this band of Freemasons from Alton and other river towns formed what was known as a "traveling military lodge" with the purpose of recruiting and initiating fellow soldiers on the march to Vera Cruz.[17] They succeeded in promoting Freemasonry in the ranks, and when Company B returned and disbanded, their members joined or started lodges in Alton, Quincy, Oquawka, Knoxville, and secretly in Galesburg. Freemasons in Galesburg met in private homes before they met openly in Lanphere's drugstore. They were few in number and they chose to keep a low profile. The city directory for Galesburg lists one lodge in 1855 but none before that year. Lanphere waited until Senator Stephen Douglas, a famous Illinois Freemason, made him postmaster before making the lodge an open attraction. The spread of Freemasonry in western Illinois and the desire of Knox students to form fraternities gave President Blanchard many reasons to be alarmed. As the population of the area grew, the lodges multiplied. In 1856 there were 185 lodges in Illinois, with more forming every year.[18] Nearby Knoxville had three Masonic chapters and two Odd Fellows; Abingdon had two Masonic lodges and one Odd Fellow. Blanchard began to see Knox College as an island in a rising tide of Freemasonry. Only hyper-vigilance could protect the Knox campus from its influence, and most of the students nominally agreed with Blanchard. They were content with one secret fraternity, Beta Theta Pi. Any more would surely attract notice. In their famous "Student's Farewell," the self-dismissed seniors endorsed Blanchard's position against secret societies but not without sounding a word of reservation and a bit of false reporting: "From the natural bent of his [Blanchard's] mind he is adverse to anything secret, and therefore strongly opposes all secret societies of any sort. There have been none in College. Many of the students do not agree with him in every particular, yet certainly they do not permit any prejudice to diminish their regard for their President."[19]

Blanchard's response to the conspicuous presence of Freemasons outside and increasingly within Galesburg was unrelenting criticism. One can speculate on the psychology of a man who reveals a looming conspiracy and awakens a community to an impending threat. Such a man seeks to be seen by others as intelligent, prescient, and important. Blanchard saw himself as a leader who would protect others from an insidious conspiracy. He never tired of warning Galesburg and Knox College about the threat of Freemasons. He neither saw nor accepted the idea that Freemasonry served the aspirations of many who wanted to be seen and acknowledged as honorable men. From his pulpit at Wheaton College, Blanchard led the reinvigorated Anti-Masonic party of 1880. When he accepted its nomination for president of the United States in 1884 at the national convention held in the Opera House in Galesburg, Illinois, he renewed the claim that Freemasons fomented the Civil War by spreading secession in the lodges, and he excoriated the trustees at Knox College for choosing Dr. Newton Bateman (1875–1892), an avowed Freemason, as their sixth president.[20] Blanchard never wavered in his opposition to Freemasonry, but he did fail in his surveillance: Ulricson built a Masonic and esoteric masterpiece under Blanchard's eye.

Ulricson had a fine example of how to do this in the work of Ithiel Town. Town is known to have embedded esoteric triangles in the brickwork of his Greek Revival facades. The office and warehouse at 211 Pearl Street (built in 1831–1832) of William Colgate, founder of what became the famous and enduring Colgate Palmolive Company, was just one of six companion buildings in the commercial district near the docks in lower New York City. This area served the heavy Hudson River–Erie Canal traffic. In 1832 Pearl Street was close to the river's edge. Both Town and Colgate envisioned a Greek Revival commercial district, like the Agora of ancient Athens. All six structures had Greek Revival elements, and all are thought to have had some kind esoteric iconography.[21] We can be certain that Ulricson saw Town's commercial buildings during his New York years, and by working for Town he probably learned of the plan for Pearl Street. Esoteric geometry, privileged numbers and ratios, and especially philosopher's stones were thought to give metaphysical and spiritual protection to buildings and artifacts. The Colgate-Town complex on Pearl Street barely escaped the Great Fire of 1835. To those who understood the insignia and designs on the Colgate buildings, no further proof of the power of talismanic architecture could be required. Entrepreneurs like William Colgate wanted their commercial trade centers to carry the marks of a higher calling. The rising business class believed that Greek Revival testified to freedom and economic opportunity. Their warehouses and storefronts must be temples of commerce, just as the government buildings of the day were the temples of democracy. For financial and practical reasons, their buildings could not have the impressive columns, pilasters, and pediments of a Greek temple, but they could and did have the much less expensive decorations of alchemical architecture. During the 1820s there was widespread interest in the Greek struggle for independence from the Ottoman Empire.

Americans identified with a revolution that they understood to be similar to their own. The proliferation of new American towns taking Greek names—Athens, Corinth, Ithaca, Sparta, etc.—and the nearly universal appeal of Greek Revival architecture attests to the extent of the new Republic's identification with Greece as the place of origin for political and commercial freedom.[22] The epitome of the union between commerce, government, and a sanctified temple in Greek Revival style appeared in 1833 when Town and Davis started work on the United States Customs House (1833–1842) on Wall Street, now the Federal Hall Memorial. It is the enduring icon of the Financial District, and at the center of the rotunda floor Town and Davis inscribed a "unity preserving" emblem in the form of a golden rectangle (see fig. 5). This building did look like a Greek temple, at least in its front facade. It was the Town and Davis version of the Parthenon, the great temple of Athena on the Acropolis. Of course, it was a temple without a statue of a god at its center. Instead it had a golden rectangle—perhaps to suggest the divine source of the sacred geometry that governed every dimension of this new American temple. The New York City that Ulricson found in 1835 was alive with the examples of Greece and its enduring claims to hold the secrets of beauty and fine architecture. This young architect drank deeply from the cup of sacred geometry and took its intoxicating possibilities to Peoria, Galesburg, and Andover.

Man of the Hour

When the Knox trustees approved Ulricson's plans for Old Main on December 25, 1855, they required that their new Main College stand between the older East Bricks (1844) and West Bricks (1845).[1] The Bricks had two and one-half stories for classes facing north and one-story dormitory wings extending southward. In an early lithograph of the campus, the facade of East Bricks has four pilasters, or faux columns. The Bricks had classical decorations because as a young man George Washington Gale, founder of the town and Knox College, had visited the University of Virginia. He was impressed with the vision of Jefferson's plans for a campus, and he departed with a belief that Jefferson's designs captured the finest points of campus architecture and planning. Gale intended to extend the similarity between Knox and Virginia by joining the Bricks with a colonnade. Had that been done, Knox College architecture would have taken a very different path.

Ulricson's plan for English Collegiate Gothic was a radical departure from Gale's vision.[2] It is possible that having multi-storied windows in a columnar order and eight Corinthian columns in the bell tower are concessions to Gale's preferences. Main College and the Bricks had to blend in some fashion. Furthermore, for Whiting Hall, Ulricson added

FIGURE 11—Old Main, East and West Bricks, photograph, circa 1883. Special Collections and Archives, Knox College Library, Galesburg, Illinois.

a porch with two Tuscan pilasters. Buildings on the Knox campus alluded to four orders: Doric, Tuscan, Ionic, and Corinthian. These wisps of the neoclassical orders may have been tokens to please Gale, or Ulricson may have been attempting to underscore Freemasonry's deep reverence for classical orders. In the rituals of the Second Degree of Freemasonry, initiates to the Fellowcraft or Journeyman stage listened to lectures on the meaning of three orders as expounded by Vitruvius. The Doric represented strength, stability, and masculinity; the Ionic symbolized elegance, grace, and femininity; and the Corinthian signaled delicacy and sophistication. Ulricson apparently wanted the Knox campus to have at least a suggestion of three orders. Gale's responses to Ulricson's plan are not known, but there can be little doubt that when Blanchard and his close friend and head of the executive committee, Flavel Bascom, endorsed Ulricson's plans for the "English Gothic style," they knew they were ending Gale's hope for a neoclassical campus.

The desire to imitate the University of Virginia, however, never completely vanished. In 1930 as the trustees labored to renovate their national landmark, Gale's dream resurfaced in an ambitious campus plan that envisioned colonnades linking new campus buildings. This plan, like the first, went no further than a drawing or two before the Depression sent it into the archives. The trials of World War II soon replaced thoughts of expanding the campus. After 1945, the need for modern dormitories, a student union, and a fine arts building eliminated thoughts of any version of the Virginia plan. National disasters seem to have periodically prevented the return of the neoclassical. The Panic of 1837 stalled all campus construction until 1844–1845, when the construction of the Bricks brought the campus to life. The Panic of 1857 began just after Main and Whiting Hall opened. It soon plunged Knox into insolvency. The Panic of 1873 delayed the construction of Alumni Hall until 1890. The years of the Great Depression nearly ended the campaign to renovate Old Main before it got under way.

From 1837 onward, the founders of the town and the college kept campus expansion on their agenda. They had to. Many "scholarships" promising free tuition to "Knox Manual Labor College" went to settlers as an enticement to purchase land and move to Galesburg. As the children of these investors made their way to college in the 1840s, Knox found itself with plenty of enrolled students, few buildings, and almost no tuition revenue. Faced with limited financial resources after 1845, the trustees had to choose between either finishing up the campus plan with a handsome colonnade to connect the Bricks or building a preparatory academy with one floor devoted to a collegiate "Female Department." The latter alternative would generate revenue and provide a steady stream of students for the college. With Galesburg's population standing only at 800 in 1846, Gale and his intrepid fellow trustees demonstrated that coeducation would be a permanent feature of the fledgling college. Coeducation was more important than a colonnade. The trustees of those early decades might have pursued the attractions of an all male college, as was the case at Virginia and many other prestigious colleges, but they didn't. The preparatory academy was all male until 1867, but Knox College from the start was coeducational.

Opportunities for expansion returned in 1855 when the railroad boom brought skyrocketing land values. The acres that Knox sold to the railroads converging on the south side of Galesburg suddenly made the college wealthy. The campus now stood between two centers of civic activity—a new passenger station on the south and the village square on the north. The population in 1852 was 1,500; in 1855 it approached 6,000. *The Bloomington Pantograph* called Galesburg "one of the most desirable places and residences in the West, . . . it has a greater amount of traffic than any town its size in the State being the crossing place of the Chicago and Burlington, and Peoria and Oquawka, and the terminus of the Northern Cross. On arrival of the trains the large depot is crowded with passengers. They rush for the ticket office and hotels. The crowds arriving and leaving, the scream of omnibus drivers, and the apple and cake boys reminds one of similar scenes at the Central Depot in Chicago."[3] Suddenly Galesburg had become a railroad nexus. This extraordinary turn of fortune gave Knox College an impressive endowment of $400,000. The sale of college land to the railroads was a windfall. The trustees advertised their new wealth in newspapers and in their college catalog with a claim to be the "third wealthiest college in the United States."[4] What had once been a quiet pastoral campus dedicated to manual labor and learning became a bustling educational center with aspirations to be the equal of Eastern institutions. Plans were made to change the college charter by dropping all references to "Manual Labor," and 1856 enrollment blossomed. The trustees sacrificed classrooms in the upper stories of the Bricks for more dormitory space. Classes moved to the parlors of faculty houses and to the home of President Blanchard. This venue increased Blanchard's popularity among the students and strengthened his hand in the continuing feud with Gale, whose frequent dyspepsia kept him out of his classroom. Students complained about his nearly perpetual absence. In 1855, the combined college and academy enrollments approached 400.

Well before the boom year of 1855, President Blanchard called for an aggressive building program. Knox must have not one but two college centers—Main College and the Female Seminary—facing each other on opposites sides of College Park. In the student literary magazines of 1856, *Knoxiana* and *Oak Leaf,* the Knox seniors repeated and endorsed Blanchard's arguments. "For several years past as wealth and population have increased in our State, ideas of taste and order have also rapidly developed. Young and ambitious institutions of learning many of them with good buildings and accommodations have arisen all around us to draw off and keep away students from Knox College. The facilities for communication with eastern institutions have become so great that a student, with a few days of travel and little expense, can place himself under the best instructors and advantages our nation can furnish for gaining an education, and the yearly cost will be little more than here in Galesburg."[5] The message is clear: without "good buildings" Knox could not compete with Eastern institutions. The seniors praised President Blanchard for promising an aggressive construction program: "When we take into consideration the fact that President Blanchard has been the principal one in the board of Trustees to advocate the policy of erecting good buildings. . . . it would be easy to see whose intentions be more conducive to the best good of the institution."⁶ All eyes were on Blanchard from 1855 onward.

Blanchard was eager, but he and the trustees got ahead of themselves when they ordered half a million bricks for Whiting Hall and Main College in 1854, well before they had adequate plans for either building. Evidently Blanchard wanted a stockpile of bricks on hand for immediate use as soon as the trustees approved a design. Blanchard turned to the Chicago firm of Olmstead and Nickolson, famous for building the First Presbyterian Church in Chicago, and he quickly embraced their "eclectic" design. Discussions about cost, delays in providing elevations, and the simple inconvenience of traveling to Chicago led to many postponements. As the towers of bricks rose higher, the Gale faction increased its criticism of the overconfident Blanchard. He couldn't deliver. The pressure on Blanchard intensified when Lombard College, Knox's crosstown rival, finished its main college in 1855. The Universalists, who built Lombard University, had always been an irritation to Knox's leaders. Since the early 1840s when George Washington Gale discovered to his shock and dismay that some of the original colonists were Universalists, he realized that his vision of a Calvinist community, unified in purpose and doctrine, would forever have a polite theological opponent. Led by the Conger and West families, the Universalists renounced predestination, eternal damnation, and punishment as incompatible with a loving and merciful God. With a cheeky independence, the Universalists set about buying land on the southwest corner of Galesburg and collecting donations from wealthy Easterners, like Benjamin Lombard, for the Illinois Liberal Institute. It later became Lombard College. To the chagrin and envy of Knox students and trustees, Lombard's main college opened in 1856.⁷ The building had twin towers, a parade of Roman arches for windows, and a central gabled roof covering a chapel. With relatively meager resources, Lombard demonstrated how efficiently a board of trustees could act when free from internal strife. Lombard's success galled President Blanchard. He disliked liberal theology in all its forms, which he associated with the heresies propagated by Unitarians, Gnostics, Transcendentalists, and Freemasons. The Universalists had stolen a march on Knox, and their success threatened the elite status of the Calvinist church and the leading Yankee families. If Knox did not have its main building soon, Gale and Blanchard would be seen as failed civic as well as academic leaders. Both factions would be seen as failures if neither could deliver new buildings. In a bid to catch up, Blanchard made several visits to the Olmstead office in 1855 seeking an affordable design plan. All were futile.

In nineteenth-century America, colleges were the creations of churches, and college presidents worked within their own religious and ethnic networks to choose architects. Today the notion of competitive bidding is the norm, but in nineteenth-century thinking, colleges turned to their coreligionists for proper designs and plans. Local examples mirrored the national practice. For Lombard College, the Universalists choose W.W. Boyington, builder of the First Universalist Church in Chicago and later the Illinois State Capitol in 1868. Bishop Philander Chase, an Episcopalian, designed Jubilee College near Brimfield, Illinois. Blanchard chose Presbyterians from Chicago. The pattern of "like hiring like" was everywhere accepted and expected. Only trusted insiders could be relied upon to include the right sort of symbols and decorations and exclude what might be offensive or heretical. Protestant architects didn't build Catholic churches; Catholics didn't build Protestant schoolhouses. Anti-Masons didn't build Masonic lodges. And Freemasons didn't build main colleges for the Anti-Masons. But that is precisely what happened at Knox College.

Blanchard and the Knox trustees had good reason to distrust architects with uncertain or unknown religious credentials. All remembered the Edgerton affair. David Edgerton, one of the original colonists, had been hired in 1847 to design and build First Church. Edgerton may have been the builder of the Bricks although this cannot be determined with accuracy. His success with the Bricks may have led to the even more important project of building the premier church of Congregationalists. First Church stood on a conspicuous location on the public square, and at 80 feet in length, with a width of 60 feet, a height of 24 feet, and tower steeple of 90 feet, it was the largest structure in the region. Knox's first commencement in 1846 was held in First Church. This commencement was a grand event that attracted nearly everyone in the town and filled every seat.[8] Shortly thereafter the town and the church recoiled in shock when Edgerton announced to his neighbors and clients that he "refused to walk with the church." He stubbornly refused to join the congregation that had employed him and straightforwardly declared that he was unconverted and saw no need for conversion. To overcome the embarrassment caused by this announcement, Blanchard took to the streets, regaling Edgerton at every corner with descriptions of his sad future in the afterlife. Blanchard engineered curbside meetings at which he reminded Edgerton of eternal damnation and warned him of ". . . the awful and sure fate awaiting him in the next world if he did not join while mercy was freely offered and the lamp held out to burn." Blanchard's characteristic doggedness and zeal, however, did not bear fruit. Edgerton held his ground, responding that he was as good a man as Blanchard was without conversion and without church attendance. This rejoinder rattled the spines of the congregation, all of whom believed that ". . . the more moral and upright a man might be the more awful his fate if he were not one of the elect."[9]

FIGURE 12— *Old Main*, Olmsted and Nickolson design, 1855, line drawing. Special Collections and Archives, Knox College Library, Galesburg, Illinois.

In Blanchard's cautious mind, the Chicago firm of Olmstead and Nickolson guaranteed that no shadow of the scandalous Edgerton affair could reappear, and Blanchard's trips to Chicago show that he was reluctant to abandon his trusted architects. Their design, which was widely circulated in Galesburg as an illustration on the city map and in the city directory, depicted an arched portico on the north facade, Gothic oriels, lattice windows, bell towers, cupolas, spires with finials, and gables.[10] Today this jumbled style is known as "associational Romanticism."[11] Its popularity on the rustic frontier reflected the fact that new colleges, like the Americans they served, lacked a tradition and a history. These cultural shortcomings were thought to have a remedy in eclectic buildings that appropriated a past and supplied a variety of missing traditions. The presence of many different styles stimulated the imagination to make contact with diverse European sources. What was utterly absent in recently settled Illinois could be imaginatively called to mind by fixing on this or that feature. A Roman arch signifies the glories of classical civilization; a Tudor oriel window, the success of the English Reformation; the gabled window, the Norman Conquest, and so on. Main College supplied an idealized past for young minds seeking a cultural history.

To twenty-first-century eyes, the Olmstead proposal invites comment only in disparaging terms. It is fatally flawed. There is no front entrance and apparently no place for one. It is a jumble of conflicting styles. With its many angular surfaces and valleys, the building could not have survived 150 years—or even fifty years—of Illinois climate. One side appears to be a church with a steeple, whereas the opposite end has the look of an English manor. The connecting middle portico makes a concession to the neoclassical while confounding the viewer with the idea that there is only one passage from wing to wing. The center has windows and trefoil finials that make a nod to the Gothic while the corners have the inlaid staggered stones that announce the Italianate. Each of three cupolas or belfries seems to signal a different college function: a chapel for worship, classes for teaching, and offices for faculty and administration. The Olmstead plan simply and unimaginatively connected the three functions in side-by-side sections. If each tower had a bell, this main college could toll a cacophony of incongruities.

On a more charitable interpretation, associational Romanticism prevents a building from being identified with a particular style, and thus the whole cannot be associated with the religious or secular origins of a style. It is not wholly Gothic, hence neither medieval nor Catholic in inspiration. It is not faithfully English and only slightly Tudor and thus succeeds in being American and patriotic. It has some Roman touches but not enough to recall the excesses of that pagan empire. The building is unappealing, but for Puritans it is safe. In having many styles, this main college had deep connections with no particular group or organization. Being eclectic, it became safely Protestant, and in being festooned with references, it became suitably didactic without asserting its own identity. Seen in this light, it is understandable why the Knox trustees collectively and publicly announced that they had agreed upon the "style" of the Olmstead building but rejected it because of the cost—over $50,000—and because Olmstead and Nickolson could not produce a satisfactory front elevation with an entrance.[12] In short, they liked the monstrosity but couldn't afford it. They circulated pictures of their main college building as soon as Lombard broke ground on their project early in 1855, but by the end of the summer, a desperate President Blanchard turned to Ulricson and asked him to submit a design. Suddenly the outsider, who was standing by to act as general contractor, became the man of the hour, and he was ready. To the surprise of everyone, Ulricson quickly submitted a completely new design in English Collegiate Gothic. An astonished but pleased executive committee listened to Ulricson's presentations and rushed to approve the new design in October 1855; the full board did the same on December 25.[13] Word of the change spread through Galesburg, and Ulricson took advantage of his notoriety by running advertisements in the local papers stating that he could offer "plans for any kind of building on short notice."[14] The trustees praised Ulricson for "extricating them from their difficulty."[15]

The building plans that Ulricson showed the executive committee in October 1855 had two sources—New York University, designed by Ithiel Town, Alexander Jackson Davis, and James Dakin in 1834 and completed by Davis on May 20, 1837, and the Wadsworth Atheneum in Hartford, Connecticut. New York University had a stunning white marble rectangular Gothic exterior with four stories, corner battlements, and two tall towers flanking a glorious curved arch with stone tracery. It occupied 180 feet on the east side of Washington Square, then known as Washington Park, and it stood next to the Dutch Reformed Church, the home church of the Presbyterians who founded the university in 1832. In 1837 Washington Park was a large open drill field on the outskirts of old New York City in an area soon to be called Greenwich Village. The impressive new building immediately became a city landmark and an icon of an expanding metropolis no longer confined to the limits of the old colonial city. Eventually this landmark launched the American Collegiate Gothic style. Although Harvard University and Kenyon College had earlier Tudor Gothic structures, New York University's location on Washington Park in the heart of a bustling metropolis meant that its University Hall attracted more attention and more visitors. It surpassed the Masonic Gothic Hall as the premier example of a public building in the Gothic style. Samuel F.B. Morse celebrated the academic castle in the romantic landscape painting *The Chapel in the Sky*. The name stuck and the building became ". . . the first important example of American Collegiate architecture. Numerous colleges and universities followed its example and adapted its features."[16] (See fig. 7.) Many could follow its example because in essence Town and Davis provided a flexible model for an academic Gothic hall. The basic outline of a central section with parallel towers, matching wings, and corner battlements could be expanded or reduced to fit any location. Free from the requirements of colonnades or quadrangles, the Collegiate Gothic could stand alone on almost any sized lot, or it could be placed in a pattern with buildings in the same style without incongruity. In the neoclassical style, as at the University of Virginia, a colonnade leads to a central templelike structure, but in a Collegiate Gothic plan, component buildings could work alone or with their companions, even ones in a different style such as that found in the Bricks. New York University proved that the Collegiate Gothic carried its own definitional references in the form of towers and crenellation. The parapets and pinnacles lead the eye around the building's outline, as if self-contained—the ideal stand-alone building for small colleges.

The Wadsworth Atheneum preserved the defining attributes of the Gothic while adding a stiff geometry that controls the front facade (see figs. 8 and 18). The whole has the look of a fortress that is relieved from its severity by the central window and the Gothic entrance. Town focused on the front while anticipating that future additions would add to the depth of the building. Because the Wadsworth faced the city green and occupied what had been a residential lot, the observer's point of view had to be straight on. The perfect balance and symmetry of Knox's Old Main represented Ulricson's creative departure from his sources. Neither New York University nor the Wadsworth offered examples of total symmetry, nor did they have peripteral windows or columns. Knox's Old Main has a rigorous geometry, but the whole effect is softer and more inviting.

When Ulricson arrived in Manhattan in 1835, New York University was the talk of the town. It signaled the expansion of the city northwards to Washington Park, and in the eyes of progressives this ended the spatial and social precedents of colonial New York. The Presbyterians who had organized and erected the new university were reformers and abolitionists eager to make an architectural statement separating them from the classical models at Columbia University. When President James Matthews and other trustees told Davis that they wanted an English Gothic style that borrowed elements from Oxford, Cambridge, and Hampton Court, they knew they were asking for a new departure in academic style. American Revival styles were not imitations of older European creations. They borrowed individual features while creating new dimensions for the facades and footprints. The result freed Gothic Revival from its associations with Catholicism and medieval Cathedral Gothic. This new kind of Gothic was safely Protestant. The gables, towers, battlements, and crockets no longer seemed a throwback to the supposed superstitions of medieval institutions. On the contrary, English Gothic became an emblem of progressive reform and thus a suitable style for antislavery colleges. After the British Parliament passed the Anti-Slavery Act of 1833, the love of things English intensified among New Yorkers, especially among abolitionists. Anglophiles wanted the Tudor Gothic style to represent their support for English leadership in the antislavery struggle.

The Chapel in the Sky opened to ringing praise from local New Yorkers precisely because it promised a connection with England. A reporter for *The New York American,* one of the city's premier newspapers, wrote, "We are pleased with this new institution for what it has done in architecture. The patronage of this noble art has been common to the English race from the earliest times, and we are more than pleased to see it rising among ourselves."[17] New York University had a large central 24 by 52 feet Gothic window commencing on the second floor and rising above the fourth floor to be crowned with a crenellated gable. The interior design, largely borrowed from chapels at Oxford and Cambridge, featured elaborate stone tracery in the windows and handsome pendants in Chapel Hall. The grand window made New York University a belvedere—a building with numerous lookout windows—with a view of Washington Park. Visitors came to the chapel to look over Washington Park. The whole was immediately proclaimed, ". . . a work of art . . . far in advance of any other in our country, a specimen of the pointed architecture of the age of Henry VII, the golden age of that style. It is florid, but not gaudy; rich, but not over-wrought. All parts are bold, prominent, and dignified."[18]

With his knowledge of New York University and the example of President Matthews's leadership in creating a new university, Ulricson could build his case on successive points of similarity between the two institutions. Knox should have a main college building that took advantage of its conspicuous location between the public square on the north and the newly opened railroad station on the south. Knox's Main College would be a landmark and a belvedere overlooking an open park, just as New York University overlooked Washington Park. The symmetry of Knox's Main College provided impressive vistas through two central windows. One view took in the public square and the surrounding churches; the opposite view took in the railroad station on the south. As seen from the city streets and by the incoming passenger trains, Main College would immediately become a landmark for the city. The Olmstead design utterly failed to take advantage of the site, and it is doubtful that Olmstead and Nickolson ever visited Galesburg. Knox's expense book shows Blanchard being paid for trips to Chicago but none for the firm to come to Galesburg. Today the description of a building as a belvedere has all but disappeared because so many tall buildings and even private residences provide sweeping vistas. To call something a belvedere today seems an unnecessary afterthought, but in 1855 the idea of a belvedere created excitement. As the tallest building in the region, Main College offered sweeping prairie views. There were no tall trees in the park, and the towering elms that created "The Way to Knox" from the square to Old Main were decades in the future. A grand central staircase ascended the south arch window. At the landing the climber turned to see the north view. On the third floor in the rhetorical room, the home to the two debating societies, Gnothautii and Adelphi, the audience sat facing the highest point in the window with a grand overview of the town. President Blanchard immediately grasped the importance of the new design. Lombard University, tucked away on the southwest corner of the city, could never be either a city landmark or a belvedere. In one fell swoop Blanchard saw how to outdo the Universalists. Furthermore, he saw how to reaffirm the abolitionist mission of the college, and he immediately understood how a second Chapel in the Sky would make Knox the equal of Eastern institutions. Others would see Blanchard as a Western version of the famous Rev. Matthews. Moreover, Ulricson's plan was affordable. Ulricson promised to build Main College for $44,000. (The actual cost reached $50,000.) Blanchard had the confidence to refute all criticism from the Gale faction regarding previous mistakes and delays. He found a way to remove the embarrassing towers of brick. Blanchard had found a winner. Of course, he had no idea that Ulricson had Masonic and esoteric themes in mind. It is unlikely that Blanchard could discern such items in the elevations. What mattered were the examples of New York University and the Atheneum. Both proved that Collegiate Gothic met the requirements of Protestant colleges. Ulricson won the privilege to work without supervision or scrutiny, but he had to agree to three resolutions passed by the trustees in December 1855: The first resolution approved the elevation (or exterior appearance), the second required that the chapel have Gothic panels as its only decoration, and a third stated that all other rooms will be "plain and painted white."[19] The resolutions said nothing about geometry or interior decorations.

Manhattan's Chapel in the Sky stood for only a short sixty years before falling to demolition in 1894. Henry James witnessed the destruction from his home on Washington Square, and he angrily denounced his fellow New Yorkers, remarking, "any . . . form of civic piety [in New York is] inevitably and forever absent."[20] In 1894 Knox's Main College was aging but still strong. The Knox trustees made their college ready for a new century with a new hip roof, central steam heat to replace coal stoves in the classrooms, a fresh coat of red paint to reclaim the tricolor, and a new name, Old Main, to touch the sentiment of legions of admirers.

The Philosopher's Stone

Ulricson's buildings have two signature features: corner niches and elaborate windows. The niches serve to mark special ratios, like the divine proportion and pi. (This will be explained in the next chapter.) The windows contain Masonic signs and esoteric geometry. In Knox's Old Main the transoms above the east and west entrances have interlocking equilateral and isosceles triangles attached to a central rectangle (see fig. 13). The base of the equilateral triangle is 14.4 inches, or one Masonic cubit.

Freemasons believe that God gave King Solomon the dimensions of the Temple in Masonic cubits, also called sacred cubits or perfect cubits (1 Kings 6:5–8). A cubit is the distance from a man's elbow to the end of the middle finger. The exact length of a sacred cubit is contested and will probably never be known, partly because there is no archaeological evidence whatsoever of Solomon's Temple. All is a matter of conjecture. In England in the eighteenth century, when many Masonic rituals and ceremonies took their present forms, the length of a Masonic cubit became 14.4 inches. Also, at this time the odd prime numbers, 3, 5, 7, and their square roots, $\sqrt{3}$, $\sqrt{5}$, $\sqrt{7}$, became the knots of the perfect cubit. In Masonic legend, King Solomon required a uniform length of measure, and he settled on a rope made of human hair knotted at 1, 3, 5, and 7 cubits. The sum of the series of knots is 16: 1+3+5+7 = 16. Sixteen is a special number for Freemasons because, according to the biblical description of Solomon's Temple, there were sixteen steps leading to the Holy of Holies, the middle chamber of the Temple. In Masonic teachings all of the Temple's dimensions and proportions were based on the Masonic cubit and the knots. Alchemical architects and Masonic builders, therefore, imitated the example of Solomon's Temple by working with a special series of numbers: 14.4, 16, 28, 56, 112, and 224. The numbers 28, 56, 112, and 224 reflect successive halves of the square root of five, one of the knots. Thus, √5 = 2.24, and half of 2.24 is 1.12, then 5.6, and 2.8. Multiplying these numbers by ten or a hundred resulted in a Masonic number series (28, 56, 112, 224). Ulricson repeatedly used these numbers as dimensions for important features. Old Main's baseline running east to west is 112 feet. Its four corner towers (now missing) stood at 56 feet. The ratio of the height of the bell tower to the diameter of its platform is approximately 2.24. The area of each of the numerous diamond squares in the upper widows is 56 square inches. At the north and south entrances, the width of the threshold is five feet six inches, and the distance between the decorative niches is 14.4 feet. A full complement of these Masonic numbers defines the dimensions of the design in the transoms above the east and west entrances to Old Main, and this strongly suggests that Ulricson intended the transoms to be his

FIGURE 13—The philosopher's stone, Masonic window, west transom. Collection of the author.

version of a philosopher's stone (see fig. 13).In the transom windows above the east and west entrances to Old Main are six isosceles triangles with sides of 16 inches and bases of 28 inches, and four with sides of 14.4 inches and bases of 16 inches. There are two equilateral triangles with sides of 14.4 inches, or one Masonic cubit. In Masonic lore the equilateral triangle, "the most perfect of figures," represents God, and the isosceles triangle stands for life.[1] The central rectangle probably alludes to Solomon's Temple and to Old Main itself. Both the Temple and Old Main were places of wisdom and piety, and both contained the sixteen steps and the middle chamber. Each triangle contributes one of its sides to the all-encompassing diamond square. In Masonic iconography and in esoteric geometry the square is a symbol of Unity or Oneness. In keeping with Thomas Taylor's Neoplatonic teaching on "the universal cement," this unity square ties together the isosceles and equilateral triangles and the central rectangle. The whole window combines Ulricson's Masonic numbers—14.4, 16, 28, and 56—in a tessellated or interlocking pattern that produces a diamond square. Put another way, the unity square supervenes on the Temple-College rectangle, the life triangle, and the deity triangle. The philosopher's stone is a splendid example of an organic geometric figure in which the contributing small triangles form an integrated whole.

The diamond square is also the symbol of Freemasonry. The emblem of American Freemasonry is the overlapping square and compass enclosing the letter *G*, which makes a double reference to God and Geometry. Remove the letter *G* and the result is a diamond square standing on one of its corners. European Freemasons prefer the compass and square without the *G*. American Freemasonry absorbed heavy doses of Neoplatonic theology and esoteric geometry. This is especially evident in the doctrines that the fundamental attribute of God is Oneness and that geometry expresses divine attributes. The Christian idea of a Triune God, when mentioned, tended to be treated as an aspect or emanation from the underlying One. These liberal doctrines appalled orthodox theologians, like Jonathan Blanchard, who found them patently heretical; however, a Freemason or a practitioner of esoteric geometry could absorb the criticisms of the orthodox with remarkable equanimity. Objections were momentary obstacles to the all-encompassing power of the One, whose emanations create and sustain all things. In geometric terms, there was nothing that could not be brought under the sway of a unity figure.[2]

Ulricson probably found examples of unity figures in the exercises of his mentor Ithiel Town and in the books of Thomas Taylor. Taylor's introduction to *Proclus' Commentaries on Euclid,* a book known to be in Town's library, contained a unity figure known in antiquity as a dodekatopos. Astrologers used the twelve house diagram for casting horoscopes. (See fig. 14.) Of the unity figure itself, apart from its astrological uses, Taylor said it contained "many general truths," and that using the dodekatopos carried a special message. "You must connect the perfect with the imperfect, the agreeing and the disagreeing, the consonant and the dissonant, and out of one all things, and out of all things one."[3] Plainly Taylor believed that this unity figure was a philosopher's stone with the power to resolve differences and reconcile opposites. Taylor's figure shows eight isosceles triangles, four equilateral triangles, a central square, and a supervening square. Ulricson adapted this figure by changing the central figure to a rectangle and adjusting the sides of the various triangles to fit the Masonic numbers. The result is two equilateral triangles and ten isosceles triangles. The similarity to a dodekatopos is strong, and the meaning of the two is nearly synonymous.

Because Ulricson was keenly aware of the discord and division between the Gale and Blanchard parties, he had a good reason to

FIGURE 14—Thomas Taylor's unity square, from "Life of Proclus" by Thomas Taylor in *Philosophical and Mathematical Commentaries of Proclus on the First Book of Euclid's Elements.* Translated by Thomas Taylor, London: Payne and Egerton, 1792.

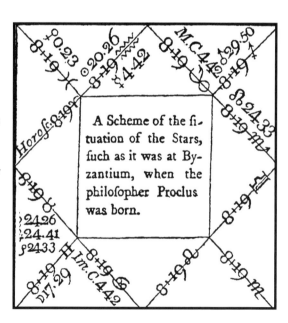

use a unity figure and its promise to reconcile differences—"out of one all things, and out of all things one." Ulricson's version of the philosopher's stone combines an intricate and ancient symbol with Masonic numbers and esoteric geometry. Perhaps Ulricson meant to signify that with the aid of God, Old Main (the temple) is the place where God and life intersect to produce piety and wisdom. Old Main would then be a place that shelters the divine-human encounter, like Solomon's Temple. This interpretation of the window is congruent with Ulricson's synthesis of Greek and Gothic themes. The union of two revival styles is another example of the power of a unity figure to reconcile or combine differences.

The idea of transforming plurality into unity, turning many into one, or the more familiar *"E Pluribus Unum,"* was a fundamental yet tenuous idea in pre–Civil War America. The years from 1820–1850 saw the creation of institutions, territories, and new states and also witnessed the forces of dissolution and division. Many Americans had a robust sense of building a new nation that would expand westward. Both Town and Davis had direct involvement in the creation of five state capitols and numerous other civic and academic buildings. One of their responses to the need to make one from many was to turn to sacred geometry. To them it was a divine science that possessed formulas to unify disparate parts. During the same period, Town and Davis saw the disestablishment of the Anglican and Puritan churches, the abolition of all vestiges of feudal law, the suppression of Freemasonry, and the emergence of nativist, abolitionist, and secessionist politics. In this period of ferment and turmoil, architects often saw their commissions to build civic and academic buildings in patriotic terms as modes of nation building. Town and Davis, and later Ulricson, turned to esoteric philosophy looking for tools and answers to the problem of forging unity. In 1857, the year Ulricson became an American citizen, the notion of a unified nation and the project of bringing new states into the Union faced grave challenges. Dissolution, not unity, became a real possibility for the country. Old Main's geometric philosopher's stone with its supervening unity square may have been Ulricson's affirmation of the Union. It graphically shows how many form one. If this was Ulricson's intention, he gave Knox College a political symbol as well as a metaphysical one. In 1860 Ulricson joined the Republican Party and supported Lincoln in his first vote as a new citizen. His daughter reported that thereafter he was a lifelong Republican.[4]

As noted earlier, Ulricson's mentor, Ithiel Town, placed a unity triangle on the facade of 211 Pearl Street, and he probably did the same on Colgate's other warehouses in the neighborhood. Town developed his unity figures using the Fibonacci series and sometimes the Masonic numbers. He and Davis used these numbers to set the dimensions of rooms in New York University. In a published plan of Ithiel Town's home and library in New Haven, Connecticut, dimensions for the library are listed as "14.375 feet." This number seems to be a covert way of referring to a Masonic cubit. It certainly attracts the attention of anyone who knows that a Masonic cubit is 14.4 inches.[5] Ulricson seems to have expanded and codified the idea of joining Masonic numbers with esoteric geometry in his projects at Knox College and Augustana. As revealed in the next chapter, all of Old Main's dimensions are multiples or whole fractions of the Masonic cubit.

When Knox students stepped through either the east or west entrances, they had to pass under the God and life triangles and the unity square. Some architectural historians refer to the Masonic practice of creating emblematic portals as "initiatory theatre" or "initiatic symbolism."[6] The central idea was to bring visitors and inhabitants into contact with sacred figures; whether this was accomplished with or without their knowledge was irrelevant to Masonic architects. Mere exposure or proximity to the ordered array of potent symbols conferred benefits. The geometric philosopher's stone operates like a charm that transforms all who pass under it. Perhaps Ulricson intended that Knox students give a silent and unknowing obeisance to Freemasonry's sacred geometric icons, or perhaps he shared the talismanic thinking that sees sacred symbols as conduits for God's creative energy and protection. One fact is clear—the transom is more than a clever decoration. From 1857–1938 there was no lantern to block the view of the transom windows; consequently, the appearance of the nexus of triangles and rectangles would have been more pronounced and more easily recognized from a distance. In planning the renovation of the interior in 1937, the building committee decided that every transom on the interior should replicate the east and west entrances. The renovation firm of Coolidge and Hodgdon liked Ulricson's design so much that without knowing the meaning of the cryptogram, they put it above every office and classroom door. Now the initiatic symbolism reigns supreme throughout the entire building, and it is impossible for any visitor or student to avoid exposure to Ulricson's philosopher's stone.

FIGURE 15—Old Main, common room window with diamond squares, photograph. Special Collections and Archives, Knox College Library, Galesburg, Illinois.

Old Main's windows hold more clues to Ulricson's design. According to some Masonic historians, the small diamond square or lozenge shape is the feminine symbol in Freemasonry. The dagger is the masculine symbol. When oaths are taken in the lodge, a dagger is placed over the diamond square. It is possible that the vertical mullion represents the dagger, and the diamond square represents the feminine lozenge shape. Perhaps the overall symbolism is a recognition and celebration of Knox's commitment to coeducation.[7] Ulricson's elaborate window designs show a remarkable degree of technical skill. In 1856 there were few craftsmen who could execute such specifications. While working on the Hall of Records in Knoxville, Ulricson met and hired A. Lofquist, an immigrant who had been a boatwright in Sweden. After settling in Knoxville in 1850, he became a skilled carpenter and eventually took the American name Clarkson.[8] The Clarkson family took pride in the fact that their ancestor made the window frames in Old Main, and with good reason. Fashioning the mullions to Ulricson's exacting specifications could not have been easy. In Knoxville, far from the eyes of the Anti-Masons, Ulricson supervised the construction of his windows. The result of the Clarkson-Ulricson collaboration is an aesthetic treasure. Old Main's windows have long been recognized as one of its principal features, and in recognition of their importance, the renovation committee in 1935–1937 took pains to make exact replicas of the original.[9]

On the interior Ulricson expanded his Masonic iconography by using the pavement of Moses and the 16 steps. The pavement of Moses is a checkerboard of black and white tiles signifying life's choices between good and evil, and it is a distinctive ornament in every Masonic lodge. Entering by the north or south meant walking on the checkerboard, just as entering from the east and west meant walking under the Masonic cryptogram in the transoms. In sum, all entrances forced the Knox student to enter under a Masonic symbol or step on one. This controlled encounter with a Masonic emblem supports the hypothesis that Ulricson intended the path to the Knox chapel on the second floor to be an initiatory theatre. The pavement of Moses led to the central staircase on the south side. Students ascended the pointed arch window by means of the "16 steps leading to the Middle Chamber" (the Knox chapel on the second floor). The metaphor of the 16 steps is the central theme in the initiation ritual of the second degree of Freemasonry, which is known as the Fellowcraft or Journeyman degree.

In that ceremony, the initiate is blindfolded, led by a towrope, and taken around the lodge in 16 edifying stops. Each stop imparts to the initiate a lesson in the liberal arts as he listens to lengthy lectures on the unity and power of God (1) and God's plan in the design of Solomon's Temple. The esoteric meaning of the lancet arch and the middle chamber are explained. Next the initiate learns the three orders of architecture: Corinthian, Ionic, and Doric (3); then the meaning of the five senses (5); and finally the seven (7) liberal arts—the Quadrivium (geometry, astronomy, arithmetic, music), and the Trivium (grammar, logic, rhetoric). Taken as a whole, the lectures recapitulate the series of numbers 1 + 3 + 5 + 7 = 16 (the sum of knots of the perfect cubit). To Freemasons the 16 steps symbolize the acquisition of a liberal arts education. Some lodges require 27 steps. These lodges add the next odd prime number (11) to the knots, and this raises the sum of knots to 27. Although we have no picture of the second flight of stairs, it is probable that it had 11 steps. To ascend the full 14 feet of the first story with a standard 6-inch rise for each step requires 27 steps—16 in the first flight and 11 in the second flight.

The symbolism of the second degree unites a Masonic view of the importance of the liberal arts with the goal of moral improvement. The Fellowcraft is in the learning stage of life, experiencing the world and structuring a life around moral goals. A liberal education supports the high purpose of crafting one's life to become a man of honor. Ulricson probably used the Fellowcraft stage as his inspiration for the interior of Old Main because it applied directly to the goals of a liberal education.[10] Old Main is, by association, the lodge for the liberal arts.

More Masonic themes are found in the north and south entrances, where heavy ashlar limestone blocks surround the north and south doors.[11] An ashlar block has a rough exterior face and a smooth top and bottom surface, which permits extremely fine joints. Old Main's ashlar blocks are the original Blue Cloud. They are some of the few pieces of stone that were not removed during the restoration. Ashlar blocks carry a deep symbolic meaning for Freemasons. Every Masonic lodge has three jewels, or key symbols, representing the craft of speculative Freemasonry.[12] They are the rough ashlar, the perfect ashlar, and the trestle board, which is a cloth or tablet displaying the symbols of Freemasonry in a summary fashion. They are tokens of the will of the Divine Architect and Geometer of the Universe.[13] There is no evidence that Old Main ever had a trestle board, but it does have

FIGURE 16—Old Main, Pavement of Moses and stairs with sixteen steps, 1936. Special Collections and Archives, Knox College Library, Galesburg, Illinois.

plenty of ashlar. The jewel of the rough ashlar is a coarse and ragged block freshly extracted from the quarry. A man enters Freemasonry a rough ashlar in need of refinement, improvement, and purification. The initiate is full of imperfections but ready for the Mason's craft. Through an esoteric alchemical process, a man can become a perfect ashlar. He passes through the degrees of Freemasonry, gives obedience to the divine architect, and does good works for his fellow men. The second jewel represents a man with a purified essence. The perfect ashlar is an exceedingly smooth stone so finely polished that it can fit with other perfect ashlars into a wall or building without mortar. The analogy between an indestructible mortarless building and the solidarity of a fraternity of morally elevated brothers is the bridge that unites operative Masonry with speculative or spiritual Freemasonry. The transition from rough to perfect ashlar captures the belief in the transformative power of the fraternity to move a man from an imperfect state, figuratively a rough stone, to a perfected spiritual being. The jewel of the ashlars (the union of operative and speculative Masonry) is the pearl of great price (Matthew 13:45–46), capturing the ideal of a Freemason as one who has raised his moral character to the highest degree of purity and perfection. Such a man will support others and be a foundation for his community.

The significance of the ashlar jewels cannot be overestimated, especially when combined with the pavement of Moses, the 16 steps, and the triangles of God and life. Ulricson's design controlled what would be called today the traffic flow, channeling all who entered into contact with the central symbols of Freemasonry and into a symbolic moral journey defined by the entrances, floor, and stairs. A visual inspection of the north and south entrances reveals that the ashlar blocks of the north entrance have rougher surfaces than their counterparts on the south entrance. Both sides show the effects of age and weathering, and both have long ago turned from blue to buttery brown; however, today the ashlar blocks on the north show deeper indentations and a rougher surface than their counterparts at the south entrance. The faces of the blocks have flaked away at a faster rate, allowing furrows to grow and multiply. The lower blocks on the north appear heavily incised. The blocks on the south are also rough, but none are as uneven as the north. Even today the brown ashlar surface slowly flakes away, exposing fresh patches of bluish gray-green Aurora limestone. The informed observer is reminded of the original appearance of floating on a blue cloud; however, the erosion of the blocks does not occur at the same rate on both entrances. The north side is far ahead of the south in its trajectory of decay.

Making one entrance rough and one smooth may have been intentional. It is possible that Ulricson selected harder and denser stones for the south while accepting softer stones for the north. Through a process known as tapping, an expert stonecutter or quarryman, like Ulricson, could "sound" a stone to determine its density. A dense block of limestone will not deteriorate as quickly as a less dense stone. When the sawed blocks arrived on site, Ulricson could have tapped each stone and sorted them according to hardness. By assigning the denser blocks to the south and the softer blocks to the north, the north side remained in a rougher state than the south. The north entrance will forever represent the rough ashlar while the south perpetually indicates the perfect ashlar. Ulricson supervised the stonework during construction, but his plan for sorting stones is unknown. The idea of the two ashlars is a conjecture supported by visual inspection, but opinions on the causes of the deteriorating stone differ. Some local stonecutters and architects argue that because the prevailing bad weather comes from the north and west, it would follow by the course of nature that the north entrance will be more severely degraded. Others claim that because the south side receives more sun and undergoes repeated cycles of expansion and contraction throughout the seasons, it should be more degraded; however, because that has not happened in the last 150 years, it may be inferred that the south entrance is comprised of the denser and harder stones.[14] Time will tell.

As with other details, Ulricson almost surely thought about the traffic patterns. The north door was the main entrance and the only acceptable entrance for women coming across College Park from the Female Seminary. The east and west entrances were partially blocked by the Bricks. Women would have shied away from those areas because the cottagelike rooms of the Bricks, each with its own door, were off-limits. The south entrance provided access to the freshwater pump, known as the pumphandle. It is difficult to imagine women being forbidden a drink and being kept off the south lawn that extended between the Bricks. The west entrance posed an obstacle for men and women because it opened directly into the chemical laboratory. As part of his strategy to construct a fire-safe building, Ulricson made the west entrance an emergency exit. Since women could not take natural science courses in the pre–Civil War Knox curriculum, the chemical laboratory and west door became part of the male domain. Probably the east door was too close to East Bricks to be used by respectable women students. Thus only the north and south entrances afforded uncontroversial portals for Knox women as they made their way to the chapel for service. In effect everyone completed the moral circuit of going through the ashlar entrances or passing under the philosopher's stone and walking on the pavement of Moses. When commencement exercises moved to the south lawn, the symbolic contrast between the two ashlars became complete. Enter by the rough stones; graduate in front of the smooth.

The Sacred Geometry

When the *Peoria Spectator* announced the opening of Old Main, it incorrectly reported the dimensions as 100 feet by 90 feet—almost a square.[1] With a baseline of 112 feet and a side of 70 feet, the footprint of Old Main is not a square but a golden rectangle. At a ratio of 112/70 it exhibits the golden ratio (1.61 to 1). The *Spectator*'s mistake may have moved Ulricson to release the dimensions of Old Main to his friend C.E. Hovey, editor of the influential journal *The Illinois Teacher*. In the fall of 1857 Hovey wrote an article on the history of Knox College to celebrate the successful completion of Main College and the Female Seminary. Hovey may have understood the importance of the dimensions of the buildings because he made a point of telling the reader that the table of dimensions came directly from Ulricson. He complimented the architect using the Platonic (and Masonic) analogy of comparing the quality of the building to the virtues of the man: "In its external proportions, Mr. Ulricson has displayed a chaste and classic taste, and added a noble edifice, while its internal appearance, its solid substantial wood work, the scrupulous attention bestowed on its immaculate finish, leave one in doubt which most to admire, the skill of the artist or the integrity of the man."[2]

Ulricson's information appears as a table in Hovey's article. Curiously, the table is set out in pairs of comparisons, as if to suggest that the reader infer the ratio for himself. It is a simple matter to complete the missing calculations and reveal the proportions of the building. The Ulricson-Hovey table, therefore, is a kind of clue inviting the mathematically inclined reader to uncover Old Main's hidden ratios. Table 6.1 replicates the Ulricson information as it appeared in *The Illinois Teacher.*[3] Table 6.2 reveals the telltale proportions.

Table 6.2 reveals that the knots of the perfect cubit ($\sqrt{3}$ and $\sqrt{5}$) and the golden ratio, 1.61 to 1, are the controlling proportions of Old Main. Proceeding in this direction suggests a comparison of *all* of the heights and widths listed in Table 6.1. The results of this exercise show still more evidence of the repeated use of the knots of the perfect cubit ($\sqrt{3}$, $\sqrt{5}$) and the golden ratio (ϕ). (See Table 6.3.)

TABLE 6.1 **Main College**

Features of building	*Measurement in feet*
Length of building	112′
Width in wings	70′
Width in centre	52′
Height of wings	53′
Height of roof in center	59′
Height of large towers	66′
Diameter of belfry octagon	14′
Height of same to top of finial	31′
Heights of stories	
First story	14′
Second story	15′
Third story	14′

Source: Information taken from C.E. Hovey, "Knox College," *The Illinois Teacher,* Vol. 3, 1857, p. 389.

TABLE 6.2 Proportions of Old Main in the Golden Ratio (φ)
and the Knots of the Perfect Cubit (√3, √5)

Dimensions	Feet	Ratio
Length of building	112′	Length/width
Width in wings	70′	112/70 = 1.6/1 = φ
Width in center	52′	Height/width = 1.01
Height of wings	53′	
Baseline	112′	Baseline/towers
Height of large towers	66′	112/66 = 1.7= √3
Diameter of belfry octagon	14′	Finial/diameter
Height of belfry octagon	31′	31/14 = 2.21 = √5
(to top of finial)		
Heights of stories		
First story	14′	Widths/sum of the stories
Second story	15′	70/43 = 1.62 = φ
Third story	14′	112/43 = 2.6 = φ²

The challenge of setting the dimensions of the heights and widths of towers, wings, center section, octagon, and bell tower in Masonic numbers must have been daunting. It is possible that Ulricson had a copy of Ithiel Town's exercises in esoteric geometry or that he had special drafting tools, such as a fixed compass with three legs set at the golden ratio or a scale of feet to cubits. All of the dimensions in Old Main are either whole cubits or thirds of a cubit. This surprising fact becomes transparent by recalculating the original Ulricson-Hovey data in Table 6.1 in terms of Masonic cubits. (See Table 6.4.)The apparent exception is the height of the belfry at 25.833 cubits; however, this anomaly can be explained by adding the height of the belfry (25.833) to the height of the building at the center (49.166). The result is 75 cubits, or 90 feet. The tallest point of Old Main could not exceed 90 feet because that was the height of the steeple of First Church. Nothing on the campus could be higher than the church on the square because

TABLE 6.3 **Width to Height Ratios Using Data from Table 6.2**

Width at center to height of bell tower	$52/31 = 1.7 = \sqrt{3}$
Height of towers to width of center	$66/52 = 1.27 = \sqrt{\phi}$
Width in wings to height of bell tower	$70/31 = 2.26 = (\approx\sqrt{5})$
Width in wings to height in wings	$70/52 = 1.32 = \frac{1}{2}\sqrt{7}$

TABLE 6.4 **Masonic Cubits in Old Main**

Dimensions	Feet	Cubits
Length of building	112′	93.333
Width in wings	70′	58.333
Width in center	52′	43.333
Height of wings	53′	44.166
Height of roof in center	59′	49.166
Height of large towers	66′	55
Diameter of belfry octagon	14′	11.666
Height to top of finial	31′	25.833

the church was the center of campus and community life. Chapel service in Old Main was part of the course of instruction. Attendance at required chapel services during the school week, which was as much a requirement as attending class, did not relieve Knox students from the obligation to attend Sunday services. Generalizing from the data in the tables, it appears that Ulricson was trying to infuse as much esoteric geometry as he possibly could into Old Main. His repeated use of the golden ratio, the knots, and the cubit is, at the least, an extraordinary technical achievement and a testament to his skill as a draftsman. It is likely that this abundance of esoteric geometry had other meanings as well.

To fully understand why the golden ratio, the Masonic cubit, and the knots of the perfect cubit are pivotal to sacred geometry, this study must take a brief digression into the metaphysics of the golden ratio. In Book VI of the *Elements,* Euclid explained how to divide or cut a line so that the whole line [a + b] stands to the larger segment [a] in the same ratio as the larger segment [a] stands to the smaller [b]. When the larger segment [a] forms the base of the rectangle with a height of [b], the result is a golden rectangle. Many psychological studies reveal a widespread human preference for golden rectangles. Aesthetic preferences are always debatable and even controversial. Still it seems no accident that the shape of many familiar objects, like the American flag, standard playing cards, and motel rooms are golden rectangles. The ubiquitous three by five notecard closely approximates a golden rectangle. Architects working in the Greek Revival style knew that the Parthenon and other famous temples and monuments in ancient Greece incorporated the golden rectangle in their features. To the practitioner of sacred geometry, the "extreme (whole) to mean (part) ratio" is a unity-preserving ratio in the sense that the ratio that governs the whole governs the division into parts: [a + b] (the whole) is to [a] (the larger part) as [a] is to [b] (the smaller part). The unity of the whole is transferred at the cut or breaking point to the sundered parts, and therefore their relationship to the original unbroken whole is preserved. The golden cut makes a division without destroying organic unity. The golden rectangle extends this reasoning by making a closed four-sided figure where the sum of the base and the height is to the base itself as the base is to the height. In Old Main adding the baseline (112) to the side (70) equals 182, which yields the ratio 182/112, or 1.62. This approximates closely the ratio of the base to the side, 112/70, or 1.61. Thus the sum of the baseline and the side [a+b] is to the baseline [a] as [a] is to the side [b]. Old Main's footprint is a golden rectangle. (See fig. 18.) Ulricson deliberately chose a golden rectangle for his masterpiece as the first step toward executing his complex plan to use Masonic numbers and sacred geometry.

For artists and architects, composing or drafting with the golden ratio and the golden cut became a way to preserve organic unity within plurality. If the artisan could assemble the parts of a composition so that they stand to each other in a golden ratio, then unity and organic wholeness permeate the entire artifact. The golden ratio artifact possesses a moral and spiritual quality that makes it both beautiful and good. Since unity is a fundamental attribute of the divine, a golden ratio object, in virtue of its unity-preserving ratios, participates in the Divine Unity. In other words, it has a piece of the divine mind in it. Practitioners of esoteric geometry believe that the golden ratio is a vehicle or conduit for God's creative energy. For this reason, scores of Renaissance artists such as da Vinci, Raphael, and Michelangelo called the golden ratio the "divine proportion."[4]

In its numeric, as opposed to its geometric, expression, the tie between the golden ratio and unity becomes even clearer. Unity, as represented by the number 1, has a unique connection with the golden ratio. The Greek letter ϕ stands for the decimal expansion of the golden ratio (i.e. 1.618+). The golden ratio is the only number whose square results by adding 1: ϕ^2= 2.618. Further, the reciprocal of ϕ is 1.618 minus 1. Thus $1/\phi$ = .618. The golden ratio is the only number whose reciprocal results by subtracting 1 and whose square results by adding 1. To an unclouded mind there is something surprising and fascinating about the connection of ϕ with the number 1. To a speculative mind searching for evidence of God in the natural and the human world, the golden ratio reveals the connections among the golden ratio, the number 1, unity, and God. The golden ratio must be more than a mere number; it must be a divine proportion and the universal cement that binds the material with the spiritual. The growth spiral of sunflowers, pinecones, and, famously, the chambered nautilus have a divine ingredient controlling and guiding their development. Similarly, when imposed on human artifacts, the universal cement fills those objects. Using the golden ratio in paintings or buildings infuses them with God's creative energy. This, in turn, shields the object with God's protective goodness. To a Masonic architect or an esoteric geometer, the visual and mathematical appeal of the golden ratio becomes by successive steps a metaphysical and quasi-religious theory of how the material and spiritual realms can be combined. Esoteric geometry is a kind of secret wisdom that converts ordinary objects into talismans. To the modern mind, the tenets of sacred geometry are examples of magical thinking. The sacred geometer indulges in sophisticated mathematical and theological rationales for believing in charms and talismans. To an alchemical architect, the special properties of the golden ratio are logical, not magical.

Understanding the appeal of the divine proportion and its remarkable transformations has a parallel in contemporary America's fascination with feng shui. The conceptual system and the cultural background of feng shui are quite different from that of esoteric geometry, but the human impulse to arrange the mundane and ordinary according to cosmic truths is strikingly similar. Both are esoteric; both link the flux of the ordinary with higher spiritual and eternal rules that do not change. Both feng shui and esoteric geometry have numerous practical applications, and both appeal to a belief in hidden order, which is logical and not magical. Both require a knowledgeable practitioner, either a sage or an artist who can transform ordinary artifacts into sacred objects with special protective or restorative powers.

In Western philosophy, esoteric geometry has its roots in Pythagoras and Plato and in the philosophies of Neoplatonism and Gnosticism. Freemasonry often acknowledges and venerates those sources as keys to understanding God, the Divine Architect and Geometer of the Universe. The geometer and the artist-architect can elevate material objects and move them toward a higher spiritual reality by setting their dimensions in the divine proportion. The golden ratio is one of God's gifts to those who understand the secrets of sacred geometry. Architects can justify their claim, as Davis phrased it, to belong to "a sacred priesthood." With sacred numbers like the golden ratio, the Masonic cubit, and pi (another number rich in lore and mysticism) architects could make a full-blown philosopher's stones, which contained many sacred numbers and ratios. These complicated talismans heighten the sense of spiritual geometry and multiply its supposed powers to transform the rough materials of art and architecture into the purified realm of divine perfection. Ulricson's attachments to Freemasonry and his exposure to Ithiel Town's teachings on the philosopher's stone go far toward explaining the repeated use of the golden ratio and the Masonic series in Old Main and Augustana Church.

To President Blanchard and the Knox trustees, the idea that geometry could somehow sanctify and protect a building by capturing a piece of the divine nature would be nothing less than geomancy, a form of necromancy and black magic. It would be a work of Satan and an abomination.[5] Making talismans smacked of animism and idolatry. For Blanchard, Ulricson's Old Main would be seen as a charm to repel evil, and, worse still, a violation of the first commandment. Further evidence of sacred geometry can be found in decoding the placements of the niches on the facades of Old Main. A careful observer will note that on the lower section the niches align with the hooded moldings over the windows, but on the upper section, which includes the second and third floors, the niches are far below the hooded moldings. In visual terms the niches punctuate the four corners and the tall towers, but in different ways. On the first floor the niches align with the window caps and reinforce the impression that one horizontal line unites all the decorative elements, but on the upper section they do not align with the caps on the windows. Obviously these placements are calculated and deliberate, but what rules of design control the placement of the niches?

In purely visual terms the niches on the upper section reduce the imposing verticality of the windows. Ulricson exploited the natural tendencies of the human eye to scan horizontally and vertically by using the niches to arrest a vertical scan while giving a viewer the starting point and a resting point for a horizontal scan. This subdues the imposing verticality of the tall multi-storied vertical windows and lets the eye form an imaginary horizontal line that corresponds to a geometric cut or division in the upper section. On the lower section the niches align with window moldings and again anchor the endpoints of a horizontal scan. A reasonable conjecture given the highly legible geometry of other features is that the niches reflect a fixed proportion, like the golden ratio. Testing this conjecture on the lower section requires careful measurements of the location of the niches relative to three separate points: the corner foundation stone, the surbase, which is the stone on top of the corner foundation stone, and the trim line, which is the horizontal line separating the lower and upper sections. It should be noted that during the restoration of the exterior in 1933–1935, the architects took pains to faithfully copy and replace nearly all the exterior features that had deteriorated since 1857. They replaced foundation stones, porch stones, hooded moldings, and trim with exact replicas in the precise locations as the originals. A few of the original hooded moldings remain, and today an observer can see that the restoration pieces match the originals. The same holds for the foundation stones and surbase stones that punctuate the four corners. As a result of the careful restoration work of 1933–1935, the exterior of Old Main today is a very close replica of the original. The measurements of the niches, foundation stones, and the surbase, as recorded in 2006, stand to each other as Ulricson actually designed them. There is one exception to an otherwise flawless restoration effort. Ulricson placed a small stone tab about nine inches square at the end of each hooded molding. These missing components can be seen in figure 17, which shows the east façade of Old Main in 1907. These tabs had the effect of heightening the perception of a horizontal line connecting niches to windows. The tabs functioned as a series of dots waiting to be connected. Ulricson probably used this device to make the visual impression of a cut or break in the lower section more pronounced. In their day the missing tabs made it almost impossible not to see the niches on the first floor as extensions of the window moldings. By contrast, the differences between the upper and lower sections, where there is no alignment between the niches and the hooded moldings, became even more noticeable. The upper section is twice the height of the lower, and two-to-one proportion mimics the division of the building into two matching wings joined by one center section. The stone trim that demarcates the lower and upper parts forms a continuous ribbon running around the building. This line unifies Old Main like a tightly wrapped package. The niches and window caps serve to divide the facades into visually more tractable subsections. The shift between unified whole to proportional parts increases the aesthetic effect of viewing Old Main. Ulricson intended the viewer to recognize the multiple ways a facade can be visually divided into parts.

Figure 17 shows the results of measuring the features of the lower section. The horizontal line *GH,* which joins all the hooded moldings and the niches, makes a golden cut in the vertical line *AC.* The length of *AC* from the surbase to the stone trim is 142 inches. The larger section, *BC,* is 88 inches. Thus 142/88 = 1.61. *BC* is 1.61 times greater than the smaller section, *AB.* The whole, *AC,* is 1.61 times greater than *BC.* In other words, the whole is to the larger part as the larger part is to the smaller. The line joining the niches and hooded moldings forms a golden ratio. When the eye moves horizontally from niche to niche, thereby connecting the window end caps with the corner niches, the observer makes a visual break in the lower section precisely at the golden ratio. Ulricson's first design rule, therefore, is this: relative to the surbase, the caps on the niches mark the golden ratio (the divine proportion).

DF/DE = π = 3.14   AC/BC ∷ BC/AB = φ = 1.61

FIGURE 17—Old Main, photograph, circa 1907, with golden ratio (φ) and pi (π) sections added. Special Collections and Archives, Knox College Library, Galesburg, Illinois.

Now for a surprise! Ignoring the surbase and turning to the distance between the foundation stones and the ends of the window caps, as represented by the vertical line *DF*, is a different ratio. The horizontal line *GH* makes a π cut in *DF*. *DF* is 170 inches, and *DE* is 54 inches. When 170 is divided by 54, the result is 3.14, or π. Ulricson's second rule reads: window caps make a π cut in the lower section relative to the foundation stones. The clever turn here is that the horizontal line *GH* is simultaneously a φ cut (at the corner niche relative to the surbase) and a π cut (relative to the window caps and the foundation stones). Ulricson found a very skilled way to make one visual horizontal scan (line *GH*) by providing two dynamic proportions, φ and π. This was no easy task because it required that Ulricson carefully coordinate the dimensions of the foundation stones and the surbase to establish two ratios. The lower section is simultaneously divided in two different ways by one horizontal line. This double dose of "geometric cutting" gives a vivid illustration of Ulricson's commitment to the belief that sacred geometry maintains unity within division.

The same two rules apply in the upper section as on the lower section. The caps on the niches make φ cuts, and the hooded moldings on the windows make π cuts; however, the horizontal lines now have different locations (see fig. 17). The two corner niches align with each other but not with the windows, as they did on the first floor. As expected, the caps on the corner niches create the φ cut in the vertical distance between the two trim lines. The hooded moldings on the windows align to create a π cut. These different cuts cannot be coordinated as they were on the first floor. Figure 18 combines all the φ and π cuts created by the niches and windows with the data from the Ulricson-Hovey table. The result is an all-encompassing net of sacred geometry with Old Main encased by the divine proportion and its kindred numbers.

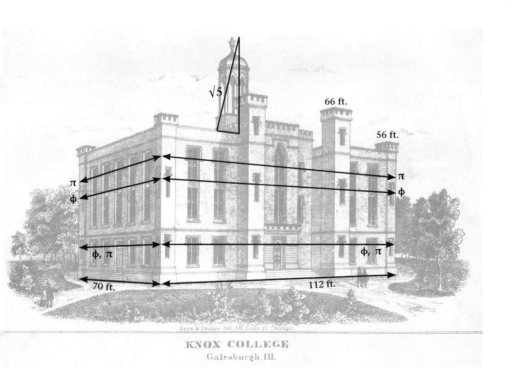

FIGURE 18—Old Main, lithograph, circa 1858, with golden ratio (φ) and pi (π) sections added. Special Collections and Archives, Knox College Library, Galesburg, Illinois.

It is evident that Ulricson's use of φ and π is carefully considered and precisely executed. Old Main has a highly legible geometry that controls horizontal and vertical scans. At the same time the ratios of sacred geometry are hidden. The building is replete with privileged ratios. All is hidden in plain sight. Ulricson could have deviated slightly from sacred geometry without destroying aesthetic appeal. Slight adjustments in the dimensions would have eliminated the divine proportion and pi without spoiling the synthesis of Greek geometry with Gothic decorations. Moreover, small modifications would have permanently removed all risk of detection. The same can be said of the Masonic cubits and the Masonic windows. Ulricson could have designed a handsome Old Main without a whisper of sacred geometry. With slight adjustments here and there, Ulricson could have protected himself from the possibility of detection and condemnation. Ulricson did not play it safe; on the contrary, he went all out to endow his masterpiece with a treasure trove of sacred geometry. Turn to any feature—the windows, the towers, the bell tower, the facades—and it is there. These features strongly suggest that Ulricson was a true believer in the power of his alchemical craft.

Like his mentor Davis, he subscribed to the doctrine that "inanimate objects have moral properties" and architects belong to a "sacred priesthood of architecture" with strict obligations to follow their esoteric convictions.[6] An alternative explanation is that he made artful choices. He relied on what he knew best, and he knew best the ways of Town and Davis. He could adapt their designs to his challenges. Ulricson may have chosen sacred geometry purely as matter of practical necessity. Faced with certain design problems resulting from his decision to combine two revival styles, he borrowed and faithfully executed Town's commitment to a precise and rigorous geometry. Ulricson's model for the rigorous geometry was Town's design for the Wadsworth Atheneum. It has a front very similar to Knox's Old Main and it, too, has hooded moldings marking off privileged ratios (see fig. 19).[7] The Wadsworth provided examples of how to create sections in a facade using the golden ratio and pi. On the artful choices hypothesis, Ulricson understood that the special ratios of sacred geometry created attractive facades. Aligning the hooded moldings made the geometric divisions highly legible. The hooded moldings, niches, and trim reinforced the impressions that the Daviséan windows were columns. Treating vertical windows as columns was crucial to making the Greek-Gothic synthesis complete. In sum Ulricson used esoteric geometry for its aesthetic effects and for its associations with the Greek Revival style. Knox's Old Main was an expansion of Town's design for the Wadsworth Atheneum without Town's convictions about the spiritual meaning and power of esoteric geometry.

At Augustana Church the golden ratio governs each of the three sections of the tower. In figure 20, the golden ratio is found in three successive sections: $BE/AB = \phi$; $AD/EF = \phi$; and $AD/AC = \phi$.[8] During the first few decades of its life, Augustana Church had spires on the corners. It is likely that the tops of the now lost spires marked a horizontal line indicating a pi cut across the front facade. The corners also have niches that define a horizontal line at C. Ulricson repeated his formula of coordinating pi and the golden ratio. The Cathedral on the Prairie is another example of the sacred geometry woven into Gothic Revival.

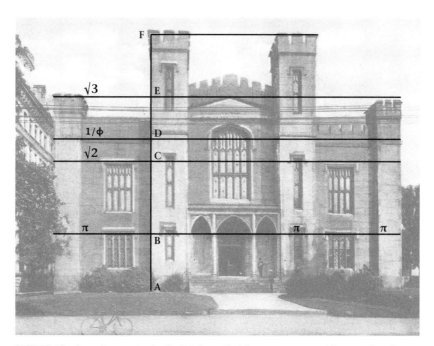

FIGURE 19—Sacred geometry in the Wadsworth Atheneum, postcard image taken from a photograph by A.C. Bosselman & Co., NY, circa 1915. Postcard in Special Collections and Archives, Knox College Library, Galesburg, Illinois.

FIGURE 20—Sacred geometry in Augustana Church, photograph, 2007. Collection of the author.

7

A Question of Style

References to Old Main's place in architectural history almost always contain qualifications. In *The Only Proper Style—Gothic Style in America,* the reader is told that Old Main ". . . displays a somewhat stiff symmetry in contrast to the more informal massing then coming into vogue."[1] Some call Old Main a "gothic castle,"[2] but for others it isn't a castle and is only slightly Gothic. In *Old Main: Fame, Fate and Contributions to Campus Planning,* the reader learns that it is only "vaguely gothic."[3] Knox's Old Main is somehow different from the numerous Gothic main halls that populate the colleges of America. The presence of Masonic elements explains some of the anomalies, but what accounts for the "vagueness," the "stiff symmetry," and the general obscurity of its Gothic credentials?

The conundrum of style is long-standing. From opening day onward, many observers raised their eyebrows, noting that Knox's Old Main is different. In 1857 the *Peoria Spectator* called the building "gothic," but at the same time the editor of the *Galesburg Free Democrat* found the bell tower objectionable because its Corinthian columns made it look too much like a "Greek temple." Classical features suggested paganism, and to some Northerners, neoclassical themes, though once popular, were now out of favor because they were far too

suggestive of the South and its detested institutions. Pagan temples in
the abolitionist stronghold of Galesburg constituted either a blunder
or an insult. Galesburg, Illinois, had earned the nickname Abolition
Hole in part by opposing Southern sympathizers in nearby Knoxville,
Illinois. The six miles between the two towns represented a division
in politics and architecture. Knoxville had a county courthouse with
a front that looked like a Greek temple.[4] For the vigilant editor of the
Galesburg Free Democrat, one temple was more than enough. To him
Old Main's bell tower tolled the wrong note.

He saw more than he knew. Ulricson intended the bell tower to be
emblematic of a synthesis of both Greek and Gothic Revival. The original
bell tower had eight Corinthian columns, complete with iron acanthus,
or thistle leaves, supporting curved Gothic arches and a wooden finial
with a thyrsus, which is a pinecone wreathed with ivy leaves. To students
of mythology and Greek religion the thyrsus is the unmistakable symbol
of Dionysus, the god of wine, passion, and revelry. When not encourag-
ing wild ecstasy, Dionysus presided over communication between the
living and the dead. In occult philosophy the thyrsus is the conduit or
transition point connecting the material and spiritual worlds. It is the
portal where the divine effluvium emanating from the all-encompassing
One enters the physical world. The Calvinists at Knox would have
been apoplectic to discover that a highly charged token of a pagan cult
crowned their Protestant schoolhouse. No doubt they accepted the idea
of a finial atop a colonnaded bell tower because lanterns and cupolas
had become immensely popular in antebellum America; however, the
normal decoration was a statue, not a thyrsus. Town, Davis, and Ulricson
favored the thyrsus, which was featured in the famous Greek monument
known as the Choragic Monument of Lysicrates in Athens (399 B.C.E.).
As one of the first monuments in antiquity to have Corinthian columns, it was prominently featured in Stuart and Revett's *The Antiquities
of Athens* (1762).[5] This book included finely crafted drawings of many
Greek monuments and temples complete with accurate measurements
of every detail of the artifacts. Its exquisite drawings made imitation
and adaptation easy and inviting; however, in post–Revolutionary
America only a few architects had copies of *The Antiquities of Athens.*[6]
Davis attributed the beginning of his career as an architect to March,
15, 1828, the day when he borrowed Town's copy of this book. In 1831
he bought it for the handsome sum of $25.00.[7] The fact that Ulricson
knew how to adapt the Choragic Monument of Lysicrates indicates that

either he had a copy of *The Antiquities of Athens* or he had sheets taken from the libraries of Town or Davis. Davis followed Stuart and Revett's drawings when he put a lantern and thyrsus finial on the top of the French Protestant Church in New York in 1832. This confident move undermined the pagan connotations of the thyrsus finial, and it became safely Protestant. Ulricson could point to the French Protestant Church and to the state capitols of Ohio, Indiana, and Illinois to defend the importance of bell towers with Greek decorations.

Ulricson's decision to combine Corinthian columns with Gothic arches was entirely novel and without precedent. It had no antecedents in Stuart and Revett's tome or anywhere else for that matter. The Greek-Gothic combination was entirely original with Ulricson, and his decision to conspicuously mix styles must be traced to alchemical architecture. His unusual bell tower signaled that Knox's Main College is a "unity of opposites" building. The synthesis of Greek and Gothic elements was completely consistent with the principles of alchemical architecture. Another consideration may have been George Washington Gale's lingering desire for a colonnade to unite East and West Bricks. The facades of the Bricks had Tuscan pilasters or faux columns. Ulricson repeated this decoration on the entrance of Whiting Hall, probably as a concession to Gale's preferences. Gale had visited the University of Virginia as a young man, and he never abandoned the idea that Jefferson's neoclassical theme was the right style for a college. Blanchard, on the other hand, had his doubts about following the precepts of Thomas Jefferson. Jefferson, who was not a Freemason, had nonetheless joined with his Masonic friends James Monroe and James Madison to participate in the Masonic rituals for laying the cornerstone for the University of Virginia on October 6, 1817. Jefferson looked on as President Monroe applied the square and plumb, just as George Washington had done at the Capitol.[8] Thereafter, Jefferson was considered a friend of Freemasons, and some Anti-Masons looked back on Jefferson's architectural examples with suspicion. Moreover, Blanchard had visited London as a participant in the Anti-Slavery Conference of 1843. There he saw Hampton Court and found the Tudor Gothic style celebrated for its connections with the creation of the Anglican Church. For Blanchard, the Tudor Gothic was an acceptable Protestant style and thus preferable to Gale's lingering hope for a neoclassical main college. On matters of style the titans were once again at odds.

Ulricson's proposal for a Greek-Gothic synthesis showed his political and artistic genius. He offered both Gale and Blanchard compelling
reasons to accept his design. The tall vertical windows hinted at being
columns; the rigorous and legible geometry captured the neoclassical
taste for harmony, symmetry, and clarity. The bell tower patriotically
referenced the lanterns and cupolas found on state capitols. On the
Gothic side there were, again, the arches of the bell tower, the tall
central belvedere windows with curved arches, towers, crenellation,
and battlements. The Knox trustees who had been to New York City
and visited the famous Chapel in the Sky or those who had been to
London and to Hampton Court found merit in Ulricson's unusual
proposal to unite two revival styles. There is nothing in Davis's lectures on architecture or his correspondence with Town to suggest
that they favored the idea of a Greek-Gothic synthesis. Davis never
blended styles or mixed decorative features. He abhorred pick-and-
choose eclecticism, which he called "meretricious." Certainly all the
revival styles were eclectic in the sense that they borrowed forms and
ornaments from the past, but the leading exponents of the revivals
from 1820–1850 were also fiercely American in their determination
to make contributions worthy of distinction and praise in their own
right. Success meant mastering a style by being a purist, not dabbling
in it as if searching for decorations. Making a style American, rather
than diluting it, became the signature of a professional. To artists
like Town and Davis, a freewheeling eclecticism signaled an indecent
broadcast of choices. Town's program of placing philosopher's stones
on or in buildings was meant to reconcile the actions and plans of
the inhabitants, not the design elements in the building. Ulricson,
however, either naively or devoutly, took the unity of opposites
theme to its logical conclusion. He saw that the principles of alchemical architecture and the power of geometric talismans extended to
the building itself. If done correctly—with precise applications of
the sacred numbers and with restraint and subtlety—the universal
cement would establish the all-encompassing unity among disparate
styles. Even the quoin blocks of the Egyptian Revival, which surround
the north and south entrances of Old Main, could find their way into
a unified whole. Thus, at one level, Ulricson's masterpiece can be
seen as a decision satisfying the competing preferences of Gale and
Blanchard, but at a deeper level it shows Ulricson taking alchemical
architecture in a new direction.

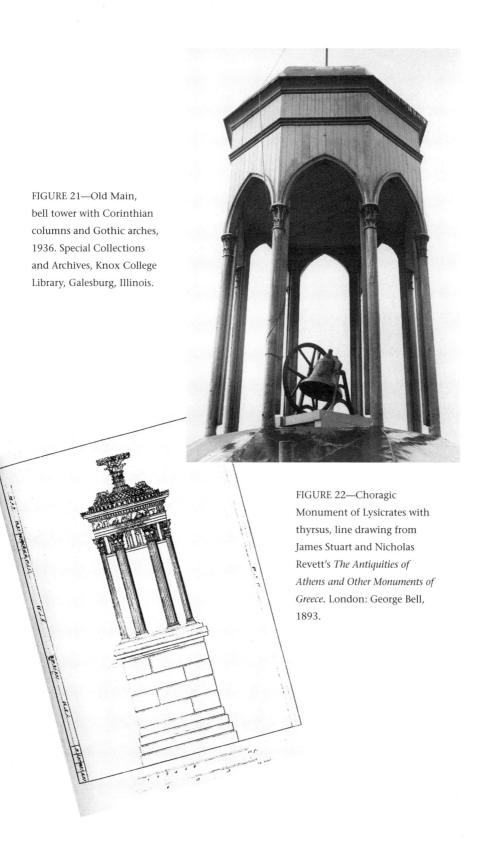

FIGURE 21—Old Main,
bell tower with Corinthian
columns and Gothic arches,
1936. Special Collections
and Archives, Knox College
Library, Galesburg, Illinois.

FIGURE 22—Choragic
Monument of Lysicrates with
thyrsus, line drawing from
James Stuart and Nicholas
Revett's *The Antiquities of
Athens and Other Monuments of
Greece*. London: George Bell,
1893.

Ulricson added another neoclassical feature to his Gothic masterpiece when he introduced the Palladian effect. Andrea Palladio (1508–1580), the leading classical revival architect in the Renaissance, popularized the innovation of having palazzo style residences display sharply juxtaposed upper and lower sections. A rusticated street level section with doors disguised as windows contrasted with a refined upper section containing columns.[9] Palladio's *The Four Books of Architecture* had enormous influence in America. Thomas Jefferson called it "the Bible," and in early nineteenth-century America, Palladio rivaled Stuart and Revett as the master source of plans and ideas. Architects experimented with different applications and versions of the Palladian effect.[10] Before the 1933 restoration, Old Main had a pronounced Palladian effect. Its lower section abounded in Blue Cloud. The porches, foundation blocks, trim, and steps displayed the rough-hewn surface of ashlar limestone. Thus the whole lower section appeared to be a dense mass supporting an elegant upper section with multi-storied columnar windows. The cambered trim dividing the first story from the upper stories marked the transition from a bumpy and knobby street level to the refined classical upper section. As the Blue Cloud aged, chipped, and flaked away, the Palladian effect increased. Perhaps this was part of Ulricson's plan. He was an expert in the various properties of Illinois River limestone. In the 1933 restoration, much of Old Main's rusticated look disappeared when five carloads of smooth cement-colored Bedford limestone from Indiana replaced nearly all of the rough stones in the foundation and porches. Today only the ashlar blocks at the north and south entrances recall Ulricson's debt to Palladio. The Palladian effect is now diminished because the exterior lacks a sharp contrast between rough and refined. Another feature attributable to Palladio is the attempt to fool the eye by treating a door as a window. On the east and west sides, the entrances mimic the proportions and outline of the flanking windows. On the upper sections the Daviséan windows with their caps suggest Ionic columns. The imposing verticality of the upper windows draws the eye upward to contemplate the temple-like bell tower and its thyrsus. In playful Gestalt-like shifts, the eye of observer can move from smooth to rough, dense to light, lower to upper, and, of course, from Gothic to Greek.

In practical terms Old Main's Daviséan windows allowed the architect to solve the problem of admitting light into the interior while creating a rhythmic effect on the exterior. In aesthetic terms Ulricson's decision to set the windows in an evenly spaced pattern that runs around the building on all four sides suggested the peripteral arrangement of a Greek temple while fulfilling the requirement of having a refined upper story to contrast with the rusticated stones on the first floor. The use of columnlike windows was a signature feature of A.J. Davis's Greek Revival buildings. He christened his innovation the Daviséan Order in a bid to win a place in the history of American architecture. Architectural historians agree that the Daviséan window system is certain evidence of his genius. Davis's biographer reported that, "It grew out of the narrow, vertical panel between pilasters and split antae so frequent along lateral faces of early Greek Revival buildings. By degrees, these casements merged with the sunken panel so as to become a single vertical unit. This Daviséan window was then spaced at regular intervals to suggest an Order [the self-named, 'Daviséan Order']. The dividing panel at floor level could be filled with a Greek fret or acanthus motif, for instance, to increase the sense of rhythm."[11] The panels at floor level added the decorative element just as capitals did for columns, and it could be repeated in horizontal and vertical patterns without loss of effect. Entire walls could be arranged to admit light and air previously unimagined. Ulricson saw the potential for putting standard floor-to-ceiling windows on the first floor while allowing soaring verticality on the upper floors as a means to recreate the Palladian contrast of rough with refined. Most architectural historians credit Davis's system as the forerunner of the vertical strip window. The received view is: "The multiple window units rose vertically through two or three stories between the piers. The interior floor levels were indicated by shallow wooden panels made flush with the glass. These were the precursors of the window wall."[12]

Ulricson made two bold changes in Davis's window system. He placed Gothic trefoils in his decorative panels, and he double hung Davis's casement windows. The result is a Daviséan Order, a hallmark of Davis's version of Greek Revival, with Gothic decorations. Davis favored casement windows for his applications of the Daviséan Order. Ulricson chose double-hung windows, and this change represents an intermediary stage between the original recessed version and the full-scale modern window wall found in skyscrapers. In aesthetic terms, the transition started at a rusticated ground level governed by the Palladian effect, then moved upward to windows as columns with Gothic panels, and finally on to a bell tower with

FIGURE 23—Old Main, photograph, 1928, east facade depicting Daviséan windows in a Daviséan Order. Special Collections and Archives, Knox College Library, Galesburg, Illinois.

Corinthian columns supporting Gothic arches and then back to a Greek decoration in the form of a thyrsus finial. Corner battlements and crenellation completed the roofline.

The first Chapel in the Sky in New York City did not have Daviséan windows, but this Midwestern version did. Ulricson fulfilled one of Davis's long-standing plans to see his signature fenestration system in a Gothic academic building. After New York University opened, Davis won commissions at the University of Michigan to build a Collegiate Gothic Hall in a large quadrangle complete with Daviséan windows on all sides. Unfortunately, the lingering effects of the Panic of 1837 ended this project without so much as a cornerstone in place. Davis was unable to demonstrate the dramatic effects of Daviséan windows arranged in a peripteral Daviséan Order. It is likely that Ulricson saw the plans for the University of Michigan and that he grasped its aesthetic impact. Ulricson, of course, understood the secret of making a window span two floors without weakening the floors and walls. Other architects didn't have Ulricson's inside knowledge; consequently, they didn't know how to overcome the problem of correcting the loads when part of the floor was exposed without support behind a thin panel. As one Davis scholar notes, the Daviséan window became ". . . such an integral part of his [Davis's] architecture that it was almost a signature. Occasionally imitated by other architects, it was too far ahead of its time to be adopted generally."[13] As a result, few examples of the Daviséan window system or its descendants survive. Most of Davis's original work, especially his windows, has been lost or radically modified. Knox's Old Main has the unique distinction of possessing a restored complete set of Daviséan windows in a Daviséan Order, exquisitely crafted by one of Davis's most able students. Today the windows fill classrooms with an abundance of light, as they were meant to do—so much so that classrooms require both blinds and shades to make use of the audiovisual equipment so popular today. In the Old Main of 1857, the chapel occupied the entire second and third floors. Nothing obstructed or absorbed the flow of light pouring in from the tall windows on three sides. The double-hung windows offered an early form of air-conditioning by allowing fetid air to escape at the top and cool air to enter from the lower window. The luminous effect in the chapel is in evidence in the 1864 photograph in figure 9. On the right in the northeast corner, an unobstructed stream of light pours through the opposing east and north windows. This is the chapel corner. For an early camera to capture this scene in 1864, a great deal of light must have been passing through two windows.

Ulricson certainly saw and probably studied the Lyceum of Natural History, which opened in 1835. The Lyceum combined a temple facade with giant pilasters on the second floor. For the ground floor Town designed the first iron storefronts in New York City, but clearly the stunning effect of the Daviséan windows between stone pilasters confirmed Davis's window innovations as the solution to letting light penetrate interior rooms and patently demonstrated how a building could accommodate large areas of glass.

For Alexander Jackson Davis, architecture was a didactic art that could edify the citizenry. He imagined a New York that emulated Periclean Athens in its power to direct a whole civilization toward progress and perfection. True to his beliefs, Davis made repeated efforts to share his library, drawings, plans, and elevations (i.e., front views drawn in perspective) with the public. During his retirement years, Davis carefully prepared scrapbooks (which are now in the Davis Manuscript Collection in the New York Public Library) partly

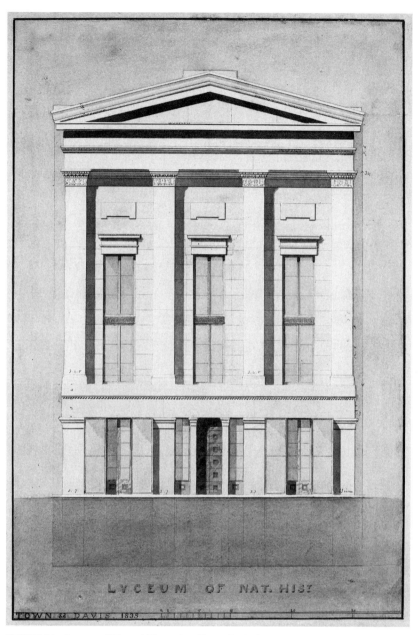

FIGURE 24—*Lyceum of Natural History* by Alexander Jackson Davis, watercolor, 1835. The Metropolitan Museum of Art, Harris Brisbane Dick Fund, 1924 (24.66.614). Image © The Metropolitan Museum of Art.

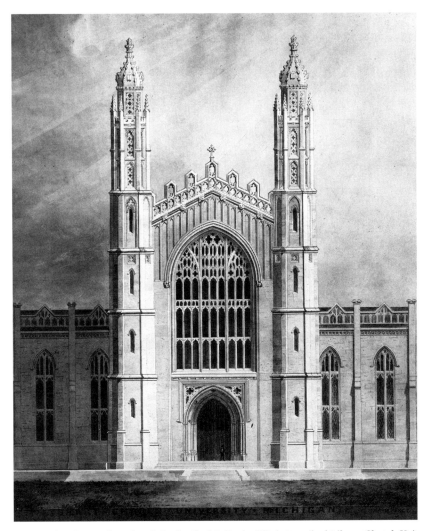

FIGURE 25—Design for a facade in the Gothic Revival Style inscribed *Library Chapel, University of Michigan*. Watercolor, ink, and graphite by Alexander Jackson Davis, 1838. The Metropolitan Museum of Art, Harris Brisbane Dick Fund, 1924 (24.66.41). Image © The Metropolitan Museum of Art.

to prove to posterity that he fulfilled the civic responsibilities of his sacred profession. Contained in the scrapbooks are Davis's advertisements inviting the public to visit his library and copy its contents.[14] Davis created what amounted to the first public architectural library in the city and invited the public to inspect, copy, ". . . and take away free of expense or questions, any part [of] his complete collection of paintings, prints and models."[15] In another advertisement he went a step further by selling copies of his plans and other material ". . . at or below cost prices" and by offering to distribute them throughout the "Union."[16] And in an even grander offer he invited the public to his salon, which he sometimes called "The Gallery of the Pantheon of Architecture," for conversation and discussion. The full text of the advertisement illustrates Davis's generosity and his enthusiasm for sharing his knowledge.

> Proprietors and those interested in Architectural Improvements may here examine models in plaster; drawings, engravings, and books, representing the most remarkable buildings of ancient and modern times with plans of public edifices and rural residences in course of execution in various parts of the U.S.; and amateurs and those building are welcome to inspect and profit, if profit they may, by said designs, plans, and collections. The Company may become known as the 'ARCHITECTURAL CONVERSAZIONE' to consist of *educated citizens and strangers of distinction invited by them*; and the object will be not only to extend a knowledge of Design and Architecture, the arts of taste and Antiquities of Design, but to learn of what improvements, and public and private works, creditable to the taste and enterprise of this country, or of cities throughout the world, are in progress of execution, either in Architecture, Sculpture, Painting, or Engineering. [Emphasis added][17]

Davis reached out to amateurs, self-educated men, gentlemen, "empirics," and indeed almost anyone with the time or inclination to learn from observation and conversation. Perhaps Ulricson was one of the strangers of distinction welcomed at the salon. During Ulricson's years in New York City, 1835–1841, Davis created in his library and office at New York University what amounted to America's first architectural classroom, complete with an open library. One can only begin to imagine how this invitation appealed to Ulricson. In Sweden the professional elites guarded their privileges and shared them only with their apprentices. The rule of the guilds and the tight control of trades and professions by families effectively kept outsiders from access to knowledge. In Sweden there was no free access to personal libraries from which to borrow or copy plans and drawings. In America, Ulricson found the nearly incomprehensible reality of free information. Davis, America's leading architect, opened his doors to permit copying and borrowing of thousands of designs! The invitation to join a salon of architectural students would be as irresistible as the offer to copy the materials in the library "at or below cost." In the "ARCHITECTURAL CONVERSAZIONE," Ulricson could ask questions, probe suggestions, extract opinions, make copies, and see examples, models, and full-scale buildings in the city. After many visits to the salon and library, Ulricson would have known the details of the celebrated Chapel in the Sky, the intricacies of the Daviséan window system, the strengths of the Town truss system, and other treasures of the firm of Town and Davis.

Davis opened his library because he believed that architects had a moral obligation to improve common values and public taste. Davis saw the destruction caused by the Great Fire of 1835 and the Panic of 1837 as opportunities for New Yorkers to rebuild and redefine their city. His office in New York University brought him into close contact with other progressives, who envisioned a new Athens on Manhattan Island. The Panic of 1837 kept tuition-paying students away from New York University, and in a desperate attempt for revenue and to save his position, President Matthews rented rooms to Davis and his professional friends. Samuel F.B. Morse moved in to open a laboratory to work on his new "telegraphic device." John W. Draper took another to experiment with photography. Samuel Colt, inventor of the revolver; Winslow Homer, painter; and William Dunlop, theatrical and artistic chronicler, also rented offices and vacant laboratories. The faculty took their offices, conversed with the new renters, and set about teaching the handful of students who did enroll. As New York University teetered on bankruptcy, President Matthews didn't hesitate to borrow money from Davis and the other artists. Davis found his loan to Matthews of $35.00 ". . . difficult to get back."[18] However, because the renters were creditors, they exercised an unprecedented degree of control over their Chapel in the Sky.[19] They set their own hours, opened their doors to patrons and to the public as they saw fit, and generally took charge of the premises. In a short time faculty became part of the public gatherings and discussions that Davis, Morse, and others organized and promoted. This concentration of professional talent became a cauldron of progressive ideas. Indeed, as one of Davis's present-day biographers observes, "It [NYU] became known as one of the cultural centers of the city and was in the avant-garde in creating in Greenwich Village a reputation and atmosphere for artistic creativity that persists to the present day."[20] Davis's open library signaled the birth of Greenwich Village as a center of discussion, populist learning, and cultural vitality. Washington Square became the place for free inquiry and for a free education in the issues of the day. Strangely and in an unpredictable way, Davis's admiration of Periclean Athens, where a city led by its architects, poets, and philosophers could educate a community, did come to fruition. Greenwich Village became the new Athens, and the white marble of New York University became Plato's Academy. Like some ancient metic, Ulricson, the eager resident alien, absorbed Greenwich Village's treasures and taught himself American ways of architecture. He stayed long enough to learn its lessons, and he copied enough to carry away plans for a new campus in faraway rustic Galesburg, Illinois.

Davis closed his NYU office in 1842 to move to the rebuilt Merchant's Exchange where he worked with Town on the Wadsworth project. When Town announced his retirement in 1842, shortly after he and Davis had completed plans for the Atheneum, Ulricson decided to strike out on his own. At the age of twenty-six, he headed south looking for a place to set up his office. It is possible that Ulricson went to New Orleans to work for James Dakin, former partner of Town and Davis. New Orleans was one of the few American cities to recover quickly from the Panic of 1837. Ulricson's daughter, Frances, reported little about her father's travels in the South except to say that he did not like its "peculiar institutions." Ulricson made his way up the Mississippi River to St. Louis and then in 1844 he settled in the boomtown of Peoria, Illinois, where there were no professional architects and certainly no contractors with Ulricson's expertise. With the Town and Davis portfolio in his portmanteau, Ulricson had a passport to the career that had been denied him in Sweden. He could show prospective clients the best designs from the leading firm in America, and the fact that he possessed such designs gave him immediate credibility. The importance of a portfolio cannot be overestimated. It was up to the architect to present what were called "compositions," or detailed pictures and elevations that could serve as catalogs and sample books for clients. In an era when architects had no institutional credentials and clients learned about important buildings either from travel or from crude drawings reproduced in newspapers, the possession of a substantial portfolio allowed architects to supply details that were otherwise unavailable. Possessing carefully sketched elevations, front views, plans, and models separated real architects from general contractors who called themselves architects. Amateurs had no portfolios. Ulricson signaled his professional standing by placing ads in the Peoria and Galesburg papers claiming that he could "promptly" produce plans and elevations for any kind of building.[21] He also followed Davis's example by opening his office in Peoria as an exhibition space for his plans and elevations.[22] He invited the public to visit his office and library to see his work, thereby confirming his professional reputation.

Over the years Knox students occasionally tried to probe the history of Old Main and resolve the puzzles associated with its windows, battlements, and bell tower. In 1890, as West Bricks came down to make way for the new Alumni Hall, some Knox students and alumni marveled at the contrast between the new and the old. Alumni Hall proclaimed the triumphs of the then popular Romanesque style, but what was the inspiration for Old Main? Some thought it must be the clock tower quadrangle at Hampton Court. Others offered Cambridge University and Westminster Cathedral. In 1927 writers for *The Knox Student* studied the window trefoils and the Gothic panels looking for European antecedents. They favored the idea that Old Main was Gothic, not Tudor. In 1930 when word of the plans for the much needed restoration spread among alumni, faculty, and administration, many took a keen interest in the history of their beloved Old Main. President Albert Britt (1925–1936) solicited memories, descriptions, and pictures of Old Main. Professor Milton Comstock, a professor of mathematics and natural science, set about measuring the bricks, trying to determine their origin. He anticipated the need for replacements and hoped to find some equivalents of the locally fired originals. Some enterprising reporters for *The Knox Student* investigated the squatty offices on the third floor of the east wing wondering why the floors there were higher than those on the west. They speculated that the original chapel must have had a high ceiling, which it did. Indeed, the chapel reached a full 29 feet, encompassing both the second and third stories. The reporters discovered to their amazement that the floor-level panels were part of one extended window.[23] No one seemed to notice that Old Main's windows are unique among academic buildings and more similar to the vertical strip windows in skyscrapers than anything found on a college campus.

In 1933 the anonymous writer of the "Town Talker" in the *Galesburg Register-Mail* canvassed local opinion on the question of style and concluded that, "Its architecture is unique for it resembles with its towers one of the ancient castles and is unlike anything here. It is one of the most striking and interesting buildings in this part of the state. It is picturesque and pleasing in outline and seems to be speaking to the character of the pioneers. It is the only building here that displays the mixed Gothic, Tudor, and Norman styles of architecture."[24] The "Town Talker" repeated what so many others found—namely, an exceedingly attractive building but one that is puzzling and not easily categorized. The whole seemed a mixture of styles but with an alchemical elixir. Its elements, though mixed, are unified and pleasing; its logic, though hidden, is dynamic and compelling. The "Town Talker" transferred her aesthetic appreciation for Old Main to an admiration for the character of the "pioneers." Apparently, Davis's doctrine of the "moral qualities of inanimate objects" had been correct, at least in this case. A building to recall the virtues of the men and women who founded the college and town is no small accomplishment.

In 1993, President John McCall (1982–1993) completed the project of repairing or replacing all of the defective bricks on the facade. At the same time, a fine senior honors project on Old Main wrestled with the problem of style. It correctly pointed to New York University as an inspiration but incorrectly linked Old Main's design with John Ruskin's *The Seven Lamps of Architecture,* published in 1850.[25] It is unlikely that the trustees or Ulricson had read Ruskin's teachings by 1855. Ulricson was simply too busy, and his education relied almost exclusively on the examples of Town and Davis, as the Daviséan window system demonstrates. Moreover, nothing in Ruskin could even remotely be taken as an approval of a Greek-Gothic synthesis. Despite Ruskin's eventual reputation as the champion of Gothic, antebellum American Revivalists disparaged the famous English critic for his lack of geometric knowledge and his failure to see the democratic qualities of Greek models. Davis found Ruskin "incoherent." To the leaders of the Greek, Gothic, Tuscan, and Egyptian revivals, Ruskin's *The Seven Lamps of Architecture* seemed an inexcusable defense of one style and thus both narrow and arbitrary. Ruskin slavishly worshiped the past. The essence of the American revival movements was an assertion of the freedom to choose from the past in order to create something entirely new and truly American. No temple in ancient Greece had a cupola, and no Gothic castle had a Daviséan Order. Ulricson learned the lessons of assertive independence from Town and Davis. He followed Town in being a purist and rigorist with respect to geometry; however, he also followed Davis in being innovative and experimental with respect to ornament and windows. He was, in short, an American architect bold enough to depart from his teachers and from the romanticism that idealized the past.

After the rededication ceremony in 1937, Old Main permanently acquired a new name—"The only *extant* site of the Lincoln Douglas debates." More correctly, it should be known as the only extant building connected to the Lincoln-Douglas debates. A site is a geographic place, and places rarely disappear, but buildings do. The semantics of "only extant site" indicate the nearly perfect elision of place, site, and edifice to form nothing less than an icon of the great debates themselves. The trajectory from Main College to Old Main to debate site to debate icon reveals the power of a national moment to overshadow architectural history and change the identity of the place it elevates to importance. Some erroneously think that Old Main was built to host the great debate, as if the plan from the outset was to make Main College the stage and bunting for an issue of enormous importance for the nation. Without an accurate architectural history to secure Old Main's unique place in the development of Collegiate Gothic, Knox's famous landmark became what it is today—a location on the Lincoln Trail.

On the east facade commemorative plaques now flank the door and invite visitors to imagine the collision between the Rail Splitter and the Little Giant, between the clash of moral law, as defended by Lincoln, and the *vox populi,* or popular sovereignty, as announced by Douglas. Regrettably, the plaques forever interfere with the aesthetic pleasure of viewing a door as a window. It is one of the ironies of history that the Palladian effect became a reality on the day of the debate, October 7, 1858. A hastily constructed platform blocked the east door and both Lincoln and Douglas had to use a window as a door to reach the debate platform. The obstacle of a window as door prompted Lincoln's (possibly apocryphal) remark, "Now I can say I have gone through college."

FIGURE 26—Commemorative Lincoln-Douglas plaques, east side of Old Main. Photograph. Collection of the author.

Over the decades numerous reenactments renewed and reinforced the connection of Knox College's Old Main with the Lincoln-Douglas debates. Arguably, October 7, 1858 became the most important day in Knox's history. Opening day, July 7, 1857, in the middle of summer with students away on holiday, never attracted attention or commemoration. To many, it was all too easy to forget that Old Main had its own story to tell. The aura of Lincoln, the martyred president who saved the Union, changed Old Main's identity. One who did not forget the tie between the building and the founding of the college was Janet Grieg Post, a graduate of the class of 1894 and Knox's first woman trustee. She became the indefatigable leader of the campaign to save Old Main. She repeatedly reminded the alumni: "The Old Main of 1937 is our tie to the Founders of 1857." She knew that the great debate mattered, but there were many other personal and individual meanings attached to this aging Chapel in the Sky that could not be captured by retellings of the Lincoln-Douglas story.

FIGURE 27—Janet Grieg Post, circa 1936. Special Collections and Archives, Knox College Library, Galesburg, Illinois.

When Ulricson died in 1877 at the age of 74, his masterpiece looked at least 74 years old, if not more, but Old Main was a young thirty. The rapid aging resulted from the natural deterioration of homemade brick. In 1844 when Gale and the trustees built West Bricks (later called Williston Hall to honor the donor, J.P. Williston), followed by East Bricks in 1845, they found local clay fired to a bright red. This happy surprise reinforced Gale's preference for choosing building materials for Main College and the Female Seminary that resembled those used at the University of Virginia. Unfortunately no one knew that in the relatively short time of two decades the bright cherry color of Old Main and Whiting Hall would leach away. Local bricks were soft and porous. Red turned to pink and then to terra-cotta. In the 1870s the trustees responded with red paint and lots of it in an attempt to preserve the cherry color of the original. In planning for Alumni Hall, the trustees chose red Colorado dolomite and redbrick to complement the red paint on Old Main but the endeavor was a losing battle. Furthermore, as blocks of Blue Cloud aged and oxidized, they turned a butternut brown and flaked away. On a sunny day, especially on the south side, when a flake falls away, a blue tint is visible, reminding the viewer that one hundred and fifty years ago Main College floated on a blue cloud. Masons plastered cement over the foundation stones and inscribed faux joints to imitate the look of mortar. They filled cracks in the porches with a cement veneer; however, cement is not blue, and paint dulls, cracks, and peels. Ivy crawled up the scabby walls. The stone trim turned pockmarked and butternut-colored. Nothing cosmetic could save the original tricolor, and it was eventually forgotten. Today only a small section of brick making up the interior wall of the attic retains the original cherry color.

By 1920 all the adventitious and cosmetic makeovers could not hide the fact that Old Main tottered toward destruction, and dangerously so. The two layers of flooring on each of the upper floors were tinder dry and flammable. The central staircase, originally designed to have students "ascend the arch" and take in vistas in all directions was, by modern standards, a chimney. With only one exit from the upper floors, Old Main had become a firetrap. Seventy years of constant use, inadequate heating, and sporadic maintenance presented the Knox trustees with a major challenge. Old Main must be renovated or destroyed. The prospect of losing Old Main appalled Janet Grieg Post. She immediately took the chair of the newly formed Restoration Committee and vowed to save Old Main from the wrecking ball. Mrs. Post must be counted as one of the noblest and most generous of Knox graduates, and she deserves to be remembered as the protector and benefactor of Old Main. Her courage, determination, and charm saved the building that truly represents the continuity of Knox College. Mrs. Post inaugurated and contributed to what became the Alumni Fund. She gave speeches, made contacts, and wrote letters and articles. She never tired of explaining the significance of saving a national landmark commemorating the fifth Lincoln-Douglas debate. She told everyone who would listen that $200,000 must be raised to save a priceless treasure. Old Main must not fall; however, by 1930, as the Great Depression deepened, the trustees faced a harsh reality. The goal could not be met, and they had no choice but to suspend the campaign. Given that Lombard College, Knox's crosstown rival, had closed its doors in 1930, their decision seemed prudent and absolute. Most alumni struggled to keep their lives going; salaries of faculty and staff had been cut; and students scrambled for odd jobs to make tuition payments. Old Main seemed doomed.

Mrs. Post responded with renewed dedication and an iron resolve as she embarked on a private and a largely silent campaign. She visited key alumni and tirelessly pursued philanthropists wherever they could be found. Her powers of persuasion must have been profound, for by 1932 she had raised enough for the college to announce that the exterior of Old Main would be accurately and meticulously restored, including a return to Ulricson's complex windows. The interior would be renovated to provide modern fireproof classrooms and offices. Restoration meant scraping paint and replacing brick. New foundations, porches, and trim required five carloads of Indiana's cementlike Bedford limestone. The absence of accurate records and pictures to guide the restoration efforts vexed the college business manager, Kellogg C. McClelland (son of President McClelland, 1900–1917). He wrote to Chicago restoration architects Coolidge and Hodgdon to report on his research on the original appearance of Old Main.[26] He assured them that Old Main originally had porches, and these must be restored with Bedford limestone; however, McClelland could find no evidence that the building ever had corner towers and a center battlement.[27] For McClelland, the Reen and Shoeber lithograph (see fig. 10) took too much artistic liberty—a fabrication of the artists not to be trusted.

Mrs. Post and former President John Finley (1892–1899), another leader of the restoration project, knew better. Their friend Edward Caldwell, a distinguished alumnus and benefactor, found and purchased the 1864 photograph that remains a fundamental point of reference for Old Main (see fig. 9). This photo brings conclusive proof to the question of battlements. Old Main had them, but because they were a problem almost from the beginning, they did not survive. In

1857 the battlements hid internal gutters that easily clogged with ice and created leaks in the roof. Roofing in 1857 was an unattractive combination of canvas covered with coal tar. In 1860 Ulricson returned to repair the plaster ceilings in the library and the chapel. The trustees paid him $350 to fix the ceiling, but the roof was still a major problem. The trustees pursued the roofing contractors in a succession of angry letters that met with equally angry responses that culminated with one contractor crying out, "Pierce your battlements!" In 1887 an enterprising Knox student offered to put lightning rods on the corner battlements and the bell tower in exchange for tuition. His proposal stated that all rods were to be connected with "solid cable" running to the ground. The college accepted his offer, but by 1893 no amount of piercing or "rodding" could save the corners, which were then dismantled and removed. At the same time Old Main got a new hip roof with a steep slope draining water to external gutters on all four sides. To raise the pitch, the roofers covered the octagon platform and removed the crenellation on the center section. After a fierce storm tore apart the hip roof on August 23, 2007, President Taylor (2001–present) approved plans for a new copper roof, and local architects Metzger and Johnson wisely exposed and sheathed the original platform in copper. Unintentionally they corrected the proportions of the bell tower and brought them close to the original. The bell tower no longer appears to spring hydra-headed from the roof, and it now stands elevated and balanced in Ulricson's original square root of five ratio. For the true believer, this proves that alchemical architecture has worked its magic and restored itself.

In 1933 the matter of the roof concerned the Restoration Committee in a number of ways. Mrs. Post quickly realized that a complete restoration including corner and center battlements with a return to Ulricson's original roof was too costly even though desirable. She very reluctantly gave up the idea of a "complete" restoration when faced with the exceedingly difficult challenge of raising money during the bitterest days of the Great Depression. Mrs. Post noted that over the years the interior had been done over many times. Returning to the original interior was neither desirable nor possible. Extensive remodeling and the requirements of an up-to-date fireproof building meant renovation on the interior, not restoration. Mrs. Post made her point with one example:

FIGURE 28—Bell tower of Old Main with copper roof and platform. Image courtesy of Peter Bailley.

> Take for example the Chapel, which was a feature of the building from 1857 to the beginning of President Finley's administration in the nineties. It occupied the east end of the second floor, extending up two stories. Soon after the building was completed more recitation room was needed, and the height of the Chapel ceiling was sacrificed. Classrooms were put above it, but the Chapel ceiling was left still a little higher than the other second floor rooms; that is why it has been necessary ever since to go up a few steps to the east rooms on the third floor.[28]

The classrooms above the chapel eventually became cramped offices connected by a warren of hallways. No one regretted the removal. Mrs. Post made a point of keeping alumni informed of restoration plans. She drew upon stories and memories of alumni that had been collected by President Britt in the 1920s. A local alumna, Myra Patch, class of 1883, remembered hearing President Bateman preaching in the (diminished) chapel. Others like Mr. Northrup, a young faculty member newly graduated from Hamilton College in 1872, recalled living in Old Main. The custodian, who carried a "very large brass key . . . locked him in the building every night."[29] Northrup became the prisoner of Old Main. A year later Northrup welcomed Henry Read, a fellow instructor, who also roomed in Old Main. For a time both men were locked in, and both had to make their way about by candlelight. Northrup and Reid shared a love of baseball; apparently the town and most of the male students did, too. Daylong games with big audiences on Saturdays filled the free space on the south lawn. The city and campus rollicked through a pastime that seemed to have no fixed rules, allowed endless innings of play, and made few distinctions among players and positions. Baseball, like the liberal arts, celebrated the freedom of aspiring amateurs.

The requirements of the 1936 renovation meant that everything had to come out: interior brick walls, tiled entryway, rock-hard pine floor joists, and the octagonal iron pillars. Workman eviscerated the building. The committee wisely saved some of the crown molding, and Dr. William L. Honnold's donations transformed the pine beams into paneling for the radiant new common room. The architects and Restoration Committee privately feared that without its iron posts and floor joists Old Main would collapse. They pondered a piecemeal renovation, but that was quickly dismissed as too expensive. The building had to be gutted front to back on all three floors to install the new interlocking steel frame. This meant removing the walls in the center section and the connecting floor joists on the upper floors. While the interior waited for its new fireproof steel cage, the exterior walls had no central support. Ulricson had made the lower brick wall three feet thick at the base to bear the weight from above, but his plan relied on two interior walls traversing the center section with floor joists running to the wings to prevent the peripheral walls from bowing out. Today there are windows tucked behind the tall towers occupying the places that once had a triple-thick layer of brick. Old Main was not one building with continuous walls but three rectangular sections standing side by side each with four walls. Without the massive brick center walls, Coolidge and Hodgdon feared the building would collapse. Structural engineers arrived to study Old Main and found it has two roofs. Ulricson's original roof supported the hip roof of 1893 with is thick rafters. The current roof adds little structurally to the soundness of the building, and in many places the older roof carries the load. The engineers determined, though not with absolute certainty, that if the bell tower temporarily came down to lessen the load, Ulricson's roof with its remarkably hard pine rafters could hold the walls together. Thus through most of 1936 and 1937, just as in the years 1856 and 1857, the fate of Old Main depended on the skill of its original designer.

At the rededication in 1937 no one mentioned the red of Old Virginia, the chapel, the Blue Cloud, the corner battlements, or the octagon. The windows were freshly painted white, but the original tricolor could not be found. The Restoration Committee took pride in the brickwork, the new grayish Bedford limestone foundation and the new hooded moldings. They exulted in a new up-to-date fireproof interior with two staircases, and for first time in its history Old Main had commodious restrooms. The privies were forever gone from the south lawn, and so was the pumphandle. Old Main now had running water. The trustees took special joy in the shining common room with its pine paneling salvaged from the beams and floorboards, the secure steel vault in the business office, ample lighting and heating throughout, and the windows. Every window, including the transoms on the east and west doors, faithfully duplicated the original. This piece of the restoration unintentionally preserved the Masonic cryptogram, and it corrected the mistake of Dr. Herbert Neal, a distinguished biology professor at the turn of the century who believed that his biology classes needed more light. He managed to have the lancet panes and mullions on the north windows removed and replaced with large panes of glass. Thankfully, Mrs. Post insisted on the original design during restoration in the 1930s. What animated discourse at the rededication was a sense of pride in a great achievement, and rightly so. In the middle of the Depression, Janet Grieg Post and the Knox alumni found a way to save a great building from almost certain destruction.

They understood that a great college should not be remembered for what it has lost but what it has saved for the future. Love of a building, a place, and a college home are deserving of respect. Architecture is an art form, as opposed to a mere practical necessity, precisely because it can alter human perceptions and inspire attachments and loyalties. Great buildings, with or without notoriety, become symbols to those who admire them, and as long as a priceless treasure endures, the community has something upon which to ground its identity. Many colleges have lost their venerable old buildings, and what replaces them seldom fosters pure devotion or preserves a bond with college memories. At the rededication of Old Main on June 15, 1937, Illinois Governor Henry Horner expressed the gratitude of past and future alumni when he said of Janet Grieg Post, ". . . that lovely lady, who attracted the eyes of a nation in her loveliness and youth, presides over us by her heart."[30] Her loyalty saved Old Main, and all Knox alumni owe a debt to Mrs. Post and her fellow donors. It is hoped that a similar confidence and determination can be found for the renovation of the mothballed Alumni Hall, another treasure waiting to welcome a new generation of students.

After the rededication, the question of style slipped away without an answer. Old Main ceased to be a building with a story of its own. It was venerable, recognizable, and admired by Knox alumni but was without a place in architectural history. Old Main's powerful friends Lincoln and Douglas propelled the popular image of Old Main along an unusual and sometimes less than flattering trajectory. The recently opened Abraham Lincoln Presidential Museum and Library in Springfield, Illinois, is a model of the now popular interactive museum design. Unlike older museums with their sometimes dusty and darkened cabinets of real objects that required visitors to squint and read, the new museum is an excursion into the world of virtual reality. Visitors to the Lincoln Museum enter a great rotunda greeted with lifelike and blemish-free mannequins. One can stand beside Lincoln or Douglas for a photograph and then move on to satellite rooms depicting different episodes in Lincoln's life. One of those rooms recreates the debate at Knox College, which shows Lincoln and Douglas standing on a platform in front of something resembling the east wall of Old Main as their background. It is shrouded in black, and the windows and door are grossly distorted. The Lincoln and Douglas mannequins gesture at the visitors as if caught in a moment of unfinished speech. Unlike other displays, this performance is silent. There are no buttons to push, no screens to bring the replicas to life, and no video to give us the substance of the debate. Ironically the great debaters are forever silent. What strikes the eye is the plastic patina of the mannequins jumping out of the black curtains that surround the exhibit. Virtual reality has its own kind of drama. The Lincoln-Douglas debate has been reduced to a frame in a comic book straining to capture the surprise of a haunted house. Old Main's ersatz windows and wall sustain the feeling of estrangement and reveal the emptiness of a debate without words. Old Main's windows are there but sadly deformed. Being covered in black drapes, they admit no light. The glories of the Greek Revival, the Palladian effect, and the Daviséan windows with their ambitious bids for illumination, clarity, and transparency are cloaked to preserve darkness. A great national landmark has at last ceased to be a building at all. In the land of virtual reality, it is black box theater. Now the puzzle is not "What style?" but "What is it?"

8

The Light in June

The bank Panic of 1857 began on August 24, 1857 with the failure of the New York office of the Ohio Trust and Insurance Company. Although it did not issue banknotes, it did issue drafts. Ohio Trust, a branch of a Cincinnati corporation, acted like a bank. It was highly reputed, and its network of circulation extending westward from Cincinnati made its "drafts" widespread in the West. St. Louis, New Orleans, and numerous smaller towns in the Mississippi River Valley had plenty of Ohio Trust paper. Galesburg was no exception, and the town and college probably had more Ohio Trust drafts and paper because the company specialized in borrowing from New York City banks in order to sell its drafts in the West, which in turn became the currency for purchasing supplies from the East.[1] Bankers in New York City knew this, and in an explosion of fear they began the liquidation of Ohio Trust paper. A desperate panic spread through the city and, propelled by the telegraph, the panic quickly jumped to St. Louis and Illinois. On August 28, the Galesburg newspapers received, and immediately published, a list of banks in the East that had failed. The *Galesburg Free Democrat* announced, "Private dispatches were received in this city from St. Louis yesterday morning containing intelligence that more of the following additional banks were yesterday thrown out in New York City." The newspaper listed banks in Maine, Rhode Island, Pennsylvania, and New Jersey. "Considerable quantities of the paper of these banks are in circulation here and not a little embarrassment and loss will ensue. The effect of this news in St Louis will excite a greater opposition than ever against all foreign currency."[2] "Foreign currency" here referred to nonlocal banks, and the implied distinction between local and nonlocal banks—the former suggested as sound and the latter not—disguised the fact that all the banks of Illinois were vulnerable. Rapidly expanding towns, like Galesburg, and colleges with ambitious building programs, like Knox, probably had plenty of Ohio Trust paper and other suspect paper passing through their accounts and hands. The panic could not be contained, and there was no immunity from the effects of worthless foreign currency.

Banks in Illinois, like other Western banks, had less gold and silver than their Eastern counterparts; accordingly, their own banknotes were heavily discounted compared with older Eastern establishments. Despite many editorial comments to the contrary, Illinois banks could not withstand a nationwide panic. When the failures of more substantial Eastern banks became widely known, Illinois banks became the immediate targets of a run. Because Illinois banks had less specie in their safes, they quickly collapsed or closed their doors. Naturally people held on to their gold and silver and refused to pay their debts in specie. They instead offered other suspect banknotes. Debtors stopped the flow of specie into banks at the same time that depositors were trying to redeem notes for gold. By the close of the year all of the banks in Illinois had failed.

The Panic of 1857 soon reduced Knox's endowment to a stack of paper. The college had little hard currency, having just paid for two handsome but expensive buildings. In June 1857, two months before the panic, the trustees took the unprecedented step, which was never repeated, of publishing their minutes as a report on the completion of Main College. No doubt the report was meant to coincide with the opening day ceremony in July. Knox's expense book for this period shows that for Main College alone the trustees had overspent by more than 10 percent. While the published report announced the cost of Main College at $44,000, its final cost came close to $50,000, and Whiting Hall, budgeted at $35,000, came in at $40,000. To keep the overruns a secret, the trustees directed the treasurer to glue together the expense book's pages relating to Main College and Whiting Hall. They remain so today. Knox's expense book contains a curious, barely visible entry in the glued section that summarizes all money expended on building Main College. Two bold lines underscore the final cost, followed by the treasurer's note reading, "This was shown to the Trustees." As the effects of the panic became noticeable, the trustees decided to hide the true cost of their building program.

The Panic of 1857 hit Knox College and the Galesburg community hard. Over the years Knox sold its land holdings in and around Galesburg to the newly arriving settlers. In effect, the college acted like a bank by extending credit in the form of land contracts. These were given out for small down payments with regular monthly payments to follow. The scheme worked well until the panic set in and debtors refused to pay on their contracts. Suddenly the college that had proudly opened two fine buildings and repeatedly declared that it was "the third wealthiest college in the nation" had no gold or silver coming into its treasury. Debts were to be paid in specie, after the banks closed. Debtors offered nothing but the now worthless paper. In a bank panic everyone hoarded whatever gold and silver they had and abandoned paper. Still, teachers and staff had to be paid, and with no cash reserve and no way to increase either tuition or enrollment, Knox College careened toward bankruptcy. The Knox trustees immediately took action to save their college. First, they sought to itemize all debts owed to the college and seek redress by threatening legal action. The problem here was that court action was expensive, time-consuming, and unlikely to produce gold and silver even if the college won its suits. The debtors simply had no money or refused to part with whatever precious metal they did have. Knox College could not sell the land that it would gain by repossession. As a result, the path of litigation and foreclosure never gained momentum. The executive committee minutes reveal the early steps of preparing cases for foreclosure, but they report no conclusive action on a single case. There was simply nothing the trustees could do to restore the college to solvency except to borrow from a bank, if one could be found, and hope that the crash would quickly pass. Like everyone else, they needed hard currency.

In the fall of 1858, the executive committee increasingly relied on the leadership of Chauncey Colton, who had led a group that brought the railroads to Galesburg, and it was widely believed that his railroad connections would be immensely useful in securing a loan. Colton convinced the trustees to hire a Chicago agent to approach banks in Boston with a proposal to offer Knox's new buildings as collateral for a loan of $10,000. Once contact was made, Colton would negotiate the terms and represent the college. The response from Jeffrey's Bank in Boston was unexpected and shocking. Their terms were harsh. Old Main and Whiting Hall were not sufficient collateral. Jeffrey's offered $10,000 at 15 percent interest if Knox pledged all of its land, buildings, and their contents as security for the loan. At first the trustees balked at the idea of putting up every stick and twig as a pledge; however, the Boston bankers would have nothing less. Colton urged quick acceptance of the terms. As the town and campus prepared for the highly anticipated debate between Lincoln and Douglas on October 7, 1858, the Knox trustees acquiesced to Jeffrey's terms. All of the college's buildings and land went down as collateral. In return the trustees received $10,000 in gold. They immediately paid the Charter Oak Bank in Hartford, Connecticut, the $3,000 they had borrowed to weather the first three months of the panic, and then they paid their Chicago agent his 5 percent commission. The trustees froze faculty salaries and cancelled orders for books, equipment, and the much-desired bell for the empty bell tower. With the remaining $6,300, Knox College prepared to wait out the panic and a devise a plan to repay their creditors. The college with the largest buildings in the West and the newest campus in the country had passed from wealth to poverty in less than a year.[3]

Throughout the panic and up to the outbreak of the Civil War, the trustees kept their financial situation a closely guarded secret. When Trustee O.H. Browning wrote Abraham Lincoln a letter on July 4, 1860, telling the new president that the faculty had awarded him Knox's first honorary degree, he made a point of mentioning the wealth of Knox College. He wrote as if the panic had not reduced the value of the endowment at all.

Dear Lincoln,

. . . Included in the last class [graduating spring of 1860] was a request to be permitted to confer the degree of L. L. D. on the Hon: Abraham Lincoln. The idea originated with the Faculty and the request was made by them without outside prompting; and having been made the Board did not think it would look well in them to refuse this honor to the President of the United States, and so the thing was ordered accordingly.

You will, therefore, after tomorrow consider yourself a "scholar" as well as a "gentleman," and deport yourself accordingly. . . . This may not be to you a very gratifying tribute, coming as it does, from a young institution just struggling for reputation, and for a place among our distinguished seats of learning. But I may say, for your comfort, that it is one of the best endowed, and destined to become one of the most useful Colleges in the land, and that after a time it will be no discredit to you that you received your degree at her hands.

We have about $210,000 in cash, loaned at 10 prct. int: whilst our entire property does not fall short of $400,000.

Truly yours,
O. H. Browning[4]

Browning's letter was meant to impress Lincoln and move him to accept the degree. This letter also indicates that the faculty had seized the opportunity of recognizing Lincoln's election as a way to end Blanchard's policy of not awarding honoraries. After Lincoln accepted the degree, the faculty established and preserved its authority to confer honors. The prohibition against honors, awards, and valedictories was forever relinquished.

During the Civil War years, Knox College continued to struggle. When the Civil War ended, nearly all of the income-producing land, what little there was, had been sold off as a means of raising cash.[5] By 1865 what Browning called the "means" of the college had fallen to below a book value of $300,000. The crisis of the Civil War and its aftermath compounded the lingering effects of the Panic of 1857. Enrollments dropped as Knox men left to join their regiments. Few returned when the war ended. The graduating class of 1862 had only three men. Twenty-three men had enlisted and gone to war. The class of 1863 had only five men, and for the first time in college history ten women joined the five men "to recite together for the first time in college and in seminary." Previously, women completed a three-year course of study in separate classes with a diploma ceremony conducted in the winter. Men completed a four-year course of study and received their bachelor's degrees in June. The class of 1863 changed that: ten women graduated on the same day and in the same commencement ceremony with five men. The trustees and faculty agreed to abandon the winter graduation and move all ceremonies to June. In addition to sharing the commencement stage, women and men were sharing classrooms and instructors in Old Main and the seminary. This meant that both sexes were making regular visits to places that had been off-limits except for rare social exchanges or for chapel meetings. Old Main now housed both women and men in the same classrooms. The fiction of being in separate courses of study could be maintained, but in reality the few men who remained were taking classes with women. The disruptions of the financial panic and those of the Civil War forced the trustees and the faculty to drop the old restrictions of gender-specific classes, at least for a time. The last barrier to truly integrated coeducation was the prohibition on granting bachelor degrees to women, and soon it was challenged. In an attempt to correct falling enrollments following the Panic of 1857, the faculty voted in June 1859 to establish a "scientific course" of study that substituted one year of German for the requirements of Latin and Greek. This change allowed the male students to earn a Bachelor of Science degree in three years. Those in the shorter course did not study any more science than those in the Bachelor of Arts program; consequently, the "scientific course" was not highly regarded.[6] Still, from the point of view of the women in the seminary and the women seeking admission to the academy, the approval of the three-year course raised the obvious question that if men could receive a bachelor's degree in three years without the study of ancient languages, why couldn't women receive the same for their three years of study, which also did not include Latin and Greek? The distinction between a diploma for women and a degree for men now seemed entirely without foundation. President Harvey Curtis (1858–1862), who was fighting a losing battle with tuberculosis and was ill so much of time that the trustees offered to put him on half pay, was inclined to agree. He was determined to bring more students into the college, and he saw the "scientific course" as a solution to the enrollment problem. His approval of the scheme tacitly acknowledged that as women moved from the Knox Academy to the Female Seminary for a three-year course of study there was no reason to deny them a bachelor's degree. When the class of 1863 departed, there were only 38 students enrolled in college classes.[7] Academy enrollment fell to 92, down from a high of 322 in 1859.

President William Curtis (1863–1868) replaced Rev. Harvey Curtis, who died in September 1862. Having two presidents with the surname Curtis back-to-back adds much confusion to Knox College history.

They can be distinguished as presidents with two different views on coeducation. President Harvey Curtis spent most of his short tenure trying to resolve the rift between the Presbyterian and Congregationalist factions on the board of trustees and in the town by using his literary skills to defend the Presbyterian claims. He ameliorated some differences simply by not making public statements on the hot political issues of the day, though he still defended Knox's Presbyterian origins. When faced with depleted classrooms, he sought practical solutions. His illness and long confinements created a vacuum in leadership, which was quickly filled by the faculty. They reversed the prohibition against honors, established a three-year course of study, and discussed ways to remodel Old Main by converting its large lecture halls into numerous small classrooms. They convinced the trustees to hire an agent to travel throughout the region to recruit students, and they urged the trustees to admit women to the academy. The faculty saw that as women moved through the academy curriculum, many would continue into the seminary. Since classes for men and women were combined after 1862, there would be more than enough students to keep the faculty fully employed.

The second President Curtis, William Curtis, took a dim view of women and men sharing the same classes and curriculum. In his mind coeducation required gender-specific classes in different courses of study culminating in different degrees and diplomas. He planned to reverse the practice that had begun in 1862, believing that the postwar years would restore the demand, on the part of men, to have a separate college. The women enrolled in the Female Seminary had an able and determined feminist as their leader. Their principal was Ada Lydia Howard (1829–1907), an 1853 graduate of Mount Holyoke College. She advocated that women take classes with men and receive a full bachelor's degree rather than a diploma. Principal Howard was joined in spirit and in deed by nearly all the women students and most of the men, though they were still few in number. President Curtis convinced the executive committee to issue a letter to Miss Howard advising her that, ". . . there are many meanings for co–education" and that she must recognize the president's authority in this matter.[8] This statement is best understood as a warning.

Ada Howard immediately rejected the "many meanings" resolution. Principal Howard, the seminary faculty, and the women of Knox understood that the "many meanings" euphemism meant a return to the old ways. Women would be forced out of Old Main's classrooms, dispossessed of their right to take classes with men, and returned to a course of study that ended with a certificate rather than a degree. They were being told to submit to President Curtis's plan to revoke the decisions of 1862. In 1867 Ada Howard challenged President Curtis by arguing repeatedly and forcefully that women were the intellectual equals of men and were deserving of the same classes and degrees as those offered to men. Women could learn Greek and Latin and graduate in four years, or they could take the scientific course and graduate in three years. Either way they were worthy of a bachelor's degree. If given the opportunity, women could excel in any subject taught exclusively to men. To prove her point and to solidify her position, Principal Howard took the unprecedented step, never repeated after her tenure, of issuing a separate college catalog for the Female Seminary. Prior to 1867, the description of the Female Seminary had been buried behind lengthy description of the all-male programs in the college and the academy. More striking still was her decision to write a separate mission statement for the women of Knox. Titled "Our Object," the mission statement asserted that the ". . . the State depends . . . intellectually and morally . . . as much upon the daughters as the sons." Miss Howard personally supervised the editing of the new catalog for the Female Seminary. When President Curtis learned of this, he ordered her to give him the galley proof. She refused. He rushed across College Park to confront her on the steps of Whiting Hall. What followed horrified even the reporter who recorded the story: "He [Curtis] seized her by the wrists to obtain forcible possession of the sheets, and she firmly resisted, in the struggle the papers were destroyed."[9] After the tussle, President Curtis retreated to his office on the second floor of Old Main. Upon reflection Curtis realized that he had crossed the invisible line that divided verbal argument from physical impropriety. After a short time, he returned to Whiting Hall to offer an apology. He stood in the foyer and asked to see Principal Howard. She refused to see him or accept his apology. Miss Ada Lydia Howard, Principal of the Knox Female Seminary, would not come out of Whiting Hall. The next day she and two seminary faculty members offered their resignations. As word of the confrontation and resignations spread, the men and women of Knox gathered around Old Main and demanded that President Curtis resign. Of course, there were few men compared to the number of women who assembled for the demonstration, but the men could make more noise, and they did precisely that. Old Main had an armory, and it was soon breached to divulge its muskets and pistols. Many Knox men had gone through cadet training, and all knew how to handle pistols and muskets. President Curtis may have been in his office on the second floor of Old Main as young college men with firearms milled about in the hallways. Curtis may have heard them making their way to the third floor rhetorical room. This room had a towrope to ring the bell and a trapdoor leading to the octagonal platform on the roof. The armed students urged one another onward until one of their number shinnied up the bell rope, opened the trapdoor, and climbed out onto the roof. Others followed, and for the first and only time in its history, Old Main appeared to be a well defended fort with rifles bristling from its battlements. From their lofty perch the protestors repeatedly rang the bell and fired their weapons into the air. Old Main had not witnessed the clamor of a demonstration since the dismissal of President Blanchard in 1857. That was mild compared to the black powder reports that filled the air over College Park in 1867. The Civil War had made gun display and gunfire an accepted form of emotional expression. Men who had not gone to war but knew its means relished the occasion to fire their muskets, presumably above the heads of admiring women assembled in front of Old Main. There is no evidence that the local magistrates tried to suppress the noise, and soon the town knew the cause of the commotion. After two days of protest and a nearly continuous occupation of the roof that coincided with the complete boycott of all classes, President Curtis offered his resignation. It was accepted without hesitation. For the trustees the thought of all Knox students leaving in protest, as the senior class had done in 1857, spelled doom for an institution with far too few students. The departure of even a few men would have effectively ended the male half of the college. Ada Howard stayed on as principal until June 1869. Her tenure was short and dramatic. Her plans to issue separate annual catalogs with an independent mission statement were abandoned by her successor, but she stayed at Knox long enough to see women in Old Main classrooms and learn that women would be admitted to the full baccalaureate curriculum beginning in 1870. After starting a school of her own in New Jersey, she went on to become the first president of the newly chartered Wellesley College in 1875 and served in that capacity until 1881. As her obituary in the *New York Times* noted, she was "the first woman college president in the world."

From 1864 onward President William Curtis sent desperate letters to the trustees reporting on insufficient operating funds and pleading with them to raise more money. In 1866 the tone of his letters reached a high fever of supplication and ended with a ringing plea: "Tell us what to do!" The trustees did not or could not find more donations, and President Curtis had no alternative but to follow the faculty's recommendation to admit women to the preparatory academy. Women clamored for admittance, and local opinion increasingly demanded it. Why should the lower school deny what the Female Seminary proudly granted? The superintendent of Knox Academy, George Churchill, who was long a supporter of uniform coeducation at all age levels, quickly grasped the relationship between supply and demand and the value of having more women students enrolled in the lower departments of the college. A burgeoning academy with both men and women students would fill the depleted classrooms in Main College. Churchill and the trustees had found a way to bring in more tuition dollars.

Low enrollments and shrinking tuition dollars were the real problems of the post–Civil War college. Few men had returned to Knox, and fewer still presented themselves for matriculation as freshmen. In 1867 Professor Churchill addressed the crisis by proposing that Old Main be remodeled to provide more classrooms for academy students. By 1867 scores of women had been admitted into the academy, and still more were requesting admission. The need for classrooms was great. The large rooms in Old Main, particularly the chemical laboratory and the philosophy lecture hall, beckoned to be remodeled and partitioned into small classrooms. The trustees quickly saw to that, and by July 1868 they went even further: Knox's glorious chapel with its soaring Daviséan windows was cut almost in half by the installation of a floor between the second and third stories. Its Gothic panels and doors were stripped out, along with other decorations that Ulricson put in the chapel. No pictures or descriptions of the original Knox chapel survive, probably because the centerpiece of Ulricson's skill and craft lasted only one decade. By 1868 the chapel had been reduced to a utilitarian meeting hall for required prayer meetings and sermons. Men and women met every day of the week in the reduced chapel. Nothing but Ulricson's original specifications bear witness to the once commodious and inspiring chapel. From an aesthetic point of view the remodeling was a disaster. Ulricson's masterpiece was radically diminished. The new third floor above the chapel obstructed the Daviséan windows and darkened the interior. Knox no longer had a chapel filled with light; indeed, the trustees had to purchase candle sconces to bring light into the darkened room. Ulricson's theme of the moral journey required a well-lit chapel as its destination. Now the chapel was often a gloomy box ill-suited for inspiration and only weakly suggestive of its original position as the middle ground between science and the humanities. From practical and economic points of view, Churchill's plan to admit women to the academy as the equals of men saved the college from ruin at the cost of ending the beauty of a chapel illuminated by Daviséan windows.

Knox men and women, academy and college students, were no longer in separate buildings. Necessity had erased the barriers imposed by gender-specific coeducation. Old Main became common ground for both sexes, and the social interactions that followed this unusual and unexpected form of integration led inexorably to the next step in full equality: Knox women agitated to receive the same degree. A certificate was no longer satisfactory and no longer reflective of what they had learned. From 1867 onward Knox women sought what the class of 1863 had by default. In 1861 Knox women had formed the Ladies Moral Improvement Society as a counterpart to the male debating societies Adelphi and Gnothautii. In true Socratic fashion Knox women debated and agitated for full educational equality with men. They sought to modify the finishing school curriculum and win permission to take classes in Greek and the natural sciences. Their discontent was recorded in trustee minutes as "depression in the Female Seminary." This insensitive remark reflects the incorrect notion that if women are dissatisfied, there is something wrong with their mental states. Discontent was as "unnatural" as it was unexpected and must be due to "depression." After the Civil War, women outnumbered men in many educational institutions. Women's study clubs, such as the Ladies Moral Improvement Society, hid a seething discontent and a manifest desire on the part of women to have the same opportunities as men. In their clubs women studied Greek and recited Book Five of Plato's *Republic,* giving special attention to the arguments for the equality of women and men and taking comfort in the fact that the greatest philosopher of antiquity defended equality between men and women. By learning Latin and Greek or by reading philosophy, women could prove that they were the intellectual equals of men.[10]

In 1868 Dr. John Gulliver (1868–1872) became Knox's fifth

president. He inherited a difficult problem, and he began his year by reporting to the trustees that there was, again, "depression in the Seminary." He recommended that "a policy of co–education be fixed and readily understood."[11] The turmoil over the meaning of coeducation had not gone away. Ada Howard's example fueled the unrest, and in 1869 the women of Knox responded with a renewed struggle. The presence of men and women in Old Main continually reminded everyone of the separate and unequal curriculum. Most of the faculty supported a change that would bring women into the same course of study and to the same terminal degree. Finally in 1870 the trustees and the faculty reached a compromise. Women were admitted to full college courses, but their classes were separately given until their senior year. Women had six years to complete the course of study. Knox's Old Main, once a symbol of a separate male college, evolved during the Civil War years to become a stage for the gradual dissolution of gender-specific education. In sacrificing the large lecture halls and the voluminous chapel to smaller classrooms, Churchill and other progressive faculty found a way to change the meaning of coeducation while preserving the financial stability of Knox College. Women saved Knox, and so did Old Main.

George Churchill proved to be an able administrator and an educational visionary. After the Civil War he led the campaign for public schools in Galesburg. Churchill had good judgment and a certain amount of insight into the complexities of human nature. He was the ideal leader to bridge the gap between academy and college and between town and gown. The board of trustees increasingly relied on Churchill and Professors Comstock and Hurd for advice. The "Great Triumvirate" of George Churchill, Milton Comstock, and Albert Hurd possessed a reservoir of teaching experience and collective wisdom that the two Curtises lacked. Both presidents were ministers. The triumvirate was solidly academic and not given to defining issues or people in theological terms. Churchill's wisdom in matters of human relationships and his tactics for dealing with the trustees can be seen in the episode known as the "weed that tastes so sweet." In 1868 Mr. Henry Bergen, an able and popular teacher in Knox Academy, let it be known that he was "a Freethinker"—a euphemism for unbeliever. Word of his apostasy spread quickly, and it alarmed the executive committee when they heard that Bergen taught his heretical beliefs to the boys in the academy. The trustees' concern swelled to outrage, and

at President Curtis's urging, they demanded that Churchill dismiss
Bergen. Principal Churchill knew that good teachers were rare, and
he couldn't afford to lose one given that enrollments in the academy
were steadily increasing. He offered to conduct an investigation of Mr.
Bergen's habits and beliefs and make a report to the executive committee. His report sets a model for prudent deflection by moving the
horrifying fear of atheism aside to confront the lesser and forgivable
flaw of addiction to tobacco.

> Prof. Churchill reported: I have seen Mr. Henry Bergen according to the
> suggestion and have conversed with him upon the points proposed. I am
> perfectly satisfied that he will prove true to any confidence we may give
> him. He well understands that as a teacher he must teach by example as
> well as precept. And will do all that he can to further the great objects in
> view by the faculty. He says that nobody can know from any conversa-
> tion had with himself that he is skeptical, or has infidel ideas. And if
> he hereto [sic] such notions he certainly should not speak them to any
> young man who should be under him as teacher. He says that as the use
> of the weed that tastes so sweet to some and whose ascending smoke is a
> pleasant incense to the young American, that he has not indulged in that
> line at all for six months and does not expect to renew the habit. He is
> willing to teach for $700. a year and will I feel confident realize to us the
> hopes we may place in him.[12]

The vexing problems of smoking and drinking among college
men had grown alarmingly in the years after Old Main opened. Free-
thinking seems not to have spread as rapidly as the sweet-smelling
weed. Because all the classrooms in the Bricks had been converted
to dormitory rooms, faculty no longer made regular visits, and the
Bricks soon developed their own rules of conduct consistent with the
interests of young men away from the control of their parents. There
was supervision but not the total suppression of exuberance, which is
the enduring characteristic of youth. In the early years of his administration, President Blanchard preached against the vices of drinking,
smoking, and gambling. He used his pulpit to publicly embarrass men
who violated the antidrinking policy, and he was especially severe on
the upperclassman who hazed freshmen by tossing them in the air with
a blanket.[13] Blanchard believed that the blanket toss was an initiation
ritual for secret societies. As the clash with Gale intensified in 1855 and

Blanchard rushed to begin work on Main College and Whiting Hall, Blanchard relaxed his surveillance of student behavior. He had little time to oversee the antics in the Bricks, and he knew that he needed the support of the men who lived there. The bustle of construction swirling around Old Main may have deflected or suspended the usual patterns of oversight. Life in the Bricks became much less restrictive, and this was eventually reflected in the student literary magazines of 1856 and 1857. Knox men wrote candid stories about dormitory life. These rebellious writers exercised a new freedom of expression. Their discussions about a plan to "self-dismiss" made them bold enough to reveal aspects of their own conduct in stories—probably with some invented incidents—that previously went unreported. When they "self-dismissed," these writers knew that there would be no penalties for writing about smoking, drinking, and hazing. As a result, there was a short period in 1856–1857 when cliché-ridden essays on "The Fall of Rome" and "The Triumph of the Reformation" yielded to revealing vignettes of college life as Knox men experienced it.

In "Sunday in the Bricks," the protagonist, Excel, wakes up in his room in the Bricks to discover that his "chum" (roommate) has left without starting a fire in the coal stove. Excel is irritated. He feels "guilty" for not having been up in time to go to Sunday chapel. That duty must be postponed. He decides to start the fire himself, grumbling at his chum's neglect, but soon he jumps back into bed waiting for the room to warm. Lying in bed, he realizes that he has the "blues." There is nothing to do in January in the Bricks. A trip to the commissary for tea, bread, and hot chocolate brings a little nourishment, but soon Excel is back in his room, still in low spirits, and without a chum to converse with Sunday morning seems endless. What to do? He fills his clay pipe and reads Edgar Allan Poe. Excel extols the pleasures of good tobacco and a good story. Nonsmokers cannot understand the delight of blowing numerous smoke rings and watching them move around the room. Still, where is his chum, and why isn't he back? There is no conversation to be had with smoke rings, and the amusing cloudy carousel cannot entertain anyone for long. It is almost time for the second church service. He will take a two-hour break from smoking and attend chapel. There the first hour is spent eyeing the "Ladies." During the second hour he tries a nap. But the preacher is too loud, and he cannot snooze. Finally the service is ended. Back in the Bricks he finds his chum and other friends in the room. They decide to drink "champagne." College life soon seems ever so much more cheerful with "champagne" on one's lips. The blues disappear. Here the editors insert a glaring footnote: "Knox students don't drink champagne and can't afford it. We drink blackberry wine and ginger wine. Freshmen have sweet apple cider, which is sometimes hard and makes them giddy." Blackberry and gingerroot are prairie plants well suited for making new wine, and it is likely that the Swedes working on Old Main or local druggist George Lanphere could readily fill all requests.

In "Smoke" the reader finds details of the "best prank ever played on Freshmen." Early in the morning four or five upperclassmen pour into the freshman's room and wake him for conversation. All five begin to smoke their pipes. One sophomore has a much-admired Chinese pipe brought by clipper ship from San Francisco. Its huge bowl with a carved face jutting forward produces thick clouds of smoke as its proud owner rapidly draws and expels deep funnels of air. All five light their pipes and begin to vigorously puff and blow smoke in an attempt to rapidly fill the room with a suffocating storm. Their goal is to induce a coughing spell in the half-awake freshman and so terrorize the tyro that he will dash from his room clad only in a nightshirt. The plan usually works because the rooms in the Bricks are small and the unsuspecting freshman is naïve, but this morning the scheme backfires. The upperclassmen puff away and the freshman coughs continuously, as intended, but the saucy sophomore with the Chinese pipe provokes his own violent coughing spell. The pipe was too big and too productive for even this experienced lover of the "weed." With eyes closed and in one convulsive cough, the sophomore bolts for the door, but he misses the exit and crashes through the adjoining window and onto the campus green.[14]

Overseeing the interactions of students increasingly occupied administrative time. Ulricson had anticipated the supervisory and surveillance roles of the president, who acted as Dean of Students as well as Chief Executive, by putting the president's office on the second floor next to the central belvedere window. There the president, acting as dean, could overlook College Park and keep an eye on the traffic between Whiting and Old Main. In the remodeled Old Main of 1868, men and women scurried about on all three floors. Previously women had been limited to a daily prayer meeting in the chapel. The new arrangement reinforced Knox's egalitarian atmosphere and set a pattern of easy and frequent access to faculty offices that continues to the present day. Although the Bricks were always a man's world, Old Main was not because women attended chapel. Women established a well-worn path between the seminary and the college, which later became a side path to "The Way To Knox." Women drew water at the pumphandle, shared strolls on wooden sidewalks, and observed the bustling train traffic along Depot Street. The Bricks were off-limits to women but easily and closely observed. In 1860, to accommodate the increased traffic in and around Old Main, the executive committee addressed the problem of the "necessaries" by ordering construction of two new brick-vaulted privies. Here separate and equal did prevail.

The Churchill plan worked well, and Knox pulled itself out of debt. Enrollments grew, and tuition dollars filled the treasury with a reserve that proved sufficient to outlast the Panic of 1873. When Alumni Hall went up in 1890–1891, the decrepit West Bricks fell to the wrecking ball. East Bricks met the same fate ten years later to make room for Davis Hall. Old Main then stood alone without its flanking satellites. As the century closed, Old Main was no longer a belvedere: a forest of campus elms obstructed views in all directions; a newly built county courthouse blocked the view of Whiting Hall; and the railroad station had moved six blocks to the northeast. In addition, an observatory stood on the south lawn. When another great panic swept across America in 1873, Knox College survived by cutting salaries and costs.

In 1870 Ulricson began work on the First Masonic Temple in Peoria. This grand undertaking occupied almost a full city block and featured two floors of commercial space with a third floor for the Freemasons and a fourth for the Odd Fellows. The Panic of 1873 kept renters away, and Ulricson's clients, many of whom were fellow Masons, could not or did not pay him the $70,000 they owed for their new temple. At the age of 57, Ulricson was broke. The Ulricson family struggled thereafter in a reduced station that was both painful and sometimes severe. In 1877, at the age of 61, Ulricson received a medal for his achievements at the Philadelphia Centennial Exposition, but although he kept an office for another ten years there were few commissions and little income. Ulricson lived on in impoverished circumstances until his death in December 1887. His strange obituary did not mention his numerous buildings in Peoria and said nothing about Knox College or Augustana Church, reporting his passing only as the loss of an "Old Settler" who had suffered setbacks in the Panic of 1873.[15] Even a few words recalling his buildings and their architectural merit might have given the Swede who lost his mother tongue a proper memorial, but sadly the Ulricson legacy passed into obscurity. Ulricson deserved to be remembered for his talent, which blossomed quickly when he came into contact with Town and Davis, and for his achievements in Illinois. Ulricson understood the possibilities implicit in Daviséan windows, esoteric geometry, and fireproof construction. The tall Daviséan windows could be stacked one upon another for as many floors as needed, and they could be adapted to any revival style. Davis placed them in the Tuscan Revival pauper's asylum (1834–1835, 1837–1839) and in the modified Greek Revival Lyceum of Natural History (1835) (see fig. 24). The Tuscan style was the most economical of all the revival styles and the most adaptable to a wide variety of uses. It required plain facades that relied on brick or stonework to highlight the windows. There were no towers, crenellation, or columns. Its limited ornamentation often went no further than a bracketed overhang to define a low sloping roof. Greek porches with pediments and pilasters could be added if funds were available. The economies of the Tuscan style were not lost on Ulricson. His commercial Italianate buildings in Peoria were adaptations of the Tuscan pattern. In Galesburg, Illinois, he completed Whiting Hall and limited the decoration to a bracketed roofline and Tuscan pilasters that flanked the central doorway. Whiting Hall's two wings have repeating vertical windows defined by a brick arch. Here Ulricson followed Davis's preferences for simple shapes free of decoration, ". . . the geometry of design in pure shapes, relying only on the repeated rhythms of the tall windows, the texture of the stone [or brick], and the shadows of the bracketed eaves to create a mood of quiet dignity."[16] Whiting Hall had to display the reserve and composure befitting a female seminary. Also, because Ulricson inherited the plans for Whiting Hall from Rev. Flavel Bascom, chair of the executive committee, and from Olmstead and Nickolson, he had no opportunity to offer a more creative interpretation of the Tuscan. Bascom considered himself an architect, and when there was a pressing need to get started on Whiting Hall in 1855 to keep pace with Lombard College, Bascom presented plans for a building that was simply too large and too expensive. Although eventually Whiting Hall grew to the size that Bascom anticipated when its wings were expanded after the Civil War, in 1855 the trustees saw that it was beyond reach. Olmstead and Nikolson did little to reduce the size or the cost, but when given the opportunity, the "prompt" Mr. Ulricson scaled down Bascom's plans, bringing them within the budget of $30,000. The redrafted version had a smaller footprint, narrow wings, and an inviting elevated porch with pilasters that echoed those on the Bricks. With its lack of decoration and its effective use of space, Whiting Hall captured the utilitarian values of the Tuscan Revival, just as Davis had prescribed. Ulricson's restraint and practical wisdom increased the trustees' confidence in their new architect.

Main College required fresh vision and truly professional talent. Neither Rev. Bascom nor any other trustee had plans waiting in their pockets, and no one on the board had the talent to even attempt a homegrown plan. Main College had to be impressive without being extravagant, and it had to be done in a different style from Whiting and Lombard. The Female Seminary was civic Tuscan, a relatively easy style to copy and recreate, but Main College must have an internal chapel, a bell tower, exterior decorations, adequate lighting and heating, and an appearance that was not easily replicated. Ulricson could indulge in the possibilities of towers and crenellation, but once again he was constrained by a budget. He used his understanding of esoteric geometry to provide a modest exterior free from ornamentation but

FIGURE 29—Whiting Hall, circa 1870. Special Collections and Archives, Knox College Library, Galesburg, Illinois.

not without appeal. There would be no oriel windows, pinnacles, or spires. Ulricson followed Davis's strict admonition: "Admit nothing that can be called meretricious, but let the character, the proportion, expression, and ornament, be that of acknowledged beauty and truth."[17] From an aesthetic point of view, Davis's firm commandments may have governed Ulricson's decision to make a Greek-Gothic synthesis. The challenge of working in two revival modes without admitting the "meretricious" display of excessive decorations in either defined Ulricson's artistic goals. The Greek components provided a way to restrain the nearly endless possibilities of ornate Gothic while Gothic battlements and crenellation added a suggestion of whimsy and romance. Before the Knox County Courthouse went up on College Park in 1886, the contrast between the Tuscan Whiting and the English Gothic Old Main was more pronounced, and before trees filled College Park an observer could readily see and compare the play of light and shadow across both buildings. Ulricson was fully aware of Davis's mature design philosophy and its central theme of using light to emphasize all geometric elements in the facade. Every season brings a different play of light and shadow across Ulricson's buildings, drawing attention to different features. Towers, windows, entrances, and porches take their turns being disclosed and hidden. His signature niches seem to capture shadows and hold them at the corners, and the same can be said for the tall towers that cast long shadows across the belvedere windows and the doors below the crenellated balcony. This is the Daviséan aesthetic at its best.

The Lutherans in Andover wanted something that resembled the Gothic churches they remembered in Sweden, but they had few resources to go beyond a basic structure with minimal decorations.[18] Ulricson offered a simplified Gothic Revival plan with a central tower and a south-facing facade with niches and brick pendants. He also incorporated a rich donation of the golden ratio where successive golden cuts stack up one upon the other. (See fig. 20.) On a sun-rich southern exposure, the rules of Daviséan aesthetic provided a way to create transient geometric highlights by letting shadows connect different parts of the brickwork. Ulricson brought the church tower forward just enough to have a vertical shadow move across the south-facing facade, just as he had done on the south side of Old Main. On long sunny days near the summer solstice, the shadow created by the central steeple tower is nearly perpendicular. It traverses the entire facade, like a sundial, moving from one brick pendant to another. At Augustana Church the aesthetic of light and shadow replaced the surprise ordinarily found in lively ornaments like gargoyles and crockets. Augustana has eight tall but narrow vertical windows on each side of the nave. The glass is set in an eight-by-eight grid of rectangular panes. The upper section of each window is a Gothic sun window with a circle within a circle. The concentric rings are divided into eight segments that converge on the small inner circle called a centrum. In Masonic lore, the point (centrum) within a circle is the astrological sign for the sun, and for Freemasons it is "an emblem to be found in every well regulated lodge, and is explained as—the *point,* the individual brother, and the *circle,* the boundary line of his duty."[19] Each one of the eight tall windows on each side of the nave had a point within a circle design at the top. It is possible that Ulricson's repeated references to the number eight corresponds to the Freemason symbol of the gauge. A gauge is a folding ruler divided into three main segments composed of eight segments each. The rule of the gauge represents the life of a Freemason, who must divide his day into eight hours to work, eight for rest and relaxation, and eight for service to humanity.[20]

Ulricson did not have complete control over the design of Augustana Church. This Cathedral on the Prairie reflected the opinions of the building committee regarding size and length of the nave. The yeoman farmers, who fired the bricks and raised its walls, took an active part in making choices about the dimensions and decorations, but Ulricson set the height of the tower and the width to maintain the square root of five proportion. The church once had spires on its corners that probably marked a pi cut, just as the niches, which are present today, mark the golden ratio. Augustana Church includes esoteric geometry and a limited dose of Masonic symbolism, and its design plan is essentially the same as Knox's Old Main—a Gothic building with the rigorous geometry of a Town and Davis Greek Revival. Davis's aesthetics of light and shadow are manifestly evident. The tower section creates long shadows that move across the front, highlighting every feature on the supporting wings. By 1891 the congregation in Andover enjoyed enough prosperity to add expensive stained glass to all 16 windows in the nave. The original glass, known as French Crystal, had soft blue and purple tints and can still be seen in the tower windows. Surprisingly, the windows of 1891, which recently have been restored to their original colors and brilliance, display three distinct and explicit Masonic symbols: the all seeing eye, the beehive, and the sower, or Hermes the messenger. Like all churches in the Swedish Synod, the Andover church officially opposed secret societies. Men who belonged to a secret fraternity were subject to excommunication and separation from the congregation. In practice, Pastor A.G. Setterdahl and the church board simply ignored the ban because by 1891 scores of men had joined a secret mutual aid fraternity using Masonic symbols and rituals known as the Ancient Order of United Workmen. Excommunication would have expelled the leading men of Augustana Church, and that was out of the question. The United Workmen had a lodge in nearby Orion, Illinois, where Rev. Setterdahl led a congregation for ten years before moving to Andover in 1888. He knew that many in his Andover congregation were United Workmen, and there was simply no way and no need to enforce the prohibition against secret societies.[21] John Jordan Upchurch founded the United Workmen society in Meadville, Pennsylvania, in 1868 as a mutual aid society. It spread rapidly among working-class men and yeoman farmers because it evolved into an effective mutual insurance company. Each member paid one dollar into a fund that returned $500 to the family of a deceased member. The United Workmen borrowed a simplified ritual of three degrees from the Freemasons but abandoned talk of God as the Divine Architect and Geometer of the Universe in favor of the language of solidarity among workers and farmers. The favorite symbols of the United Workmen were the anchor (representing hope), the beehive (standing for industrious work), and the all seeing eye of providence. These symbols appear prominently in Augustana Church alongside the traditional Christian symbols of the dove, the crown of Christ, and the cross. In much the same way that Ulricson ignored his Yankee clients in Galesburg, the United Workmen on the building committee ignored their synod's official policy prohibiting Masonic signs. The result is a Lutheran church unlike any other in America, twice infused with the vocabulary of Freemasonry.

This account of Ulricson's alchemical architecture began with a surprising irony. It is fitting that it should end with another. The Daviséan aesthetic requires that the architect artfully control the relationships among light and shadow on exterior features. This interplay is nowhere more evident than on the south facade of Knox's Old Main. Indeed it is there that the observer can find evidence of Ulricson's attachment to the occult and thus the greatest mystery in

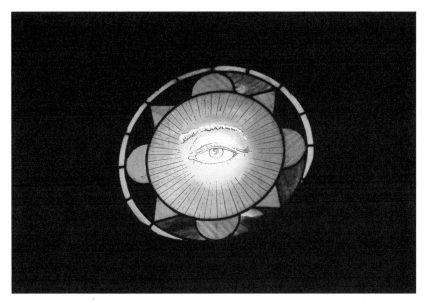

FIGURE 30—All Seeing Eye, Augustana Church. Collection of the author.

his geometric designs. On and around the summer solstice during the longest days of the year, an observer of Old Main's south wall will see a remarkable display of light and shadow. The tall towers create a long shadow that reaches and covers the opposing wall in a sharply defined right triangle with a hypotenuse of 66.6 feet long. The base of this large triangle is 36 feet and the height is 56 feet (see fig. 31). It is likely that Ulricson ingeniously placed the tall towers, which cast the shadows across the center section so that they protrude from the wall (about 7.5 feet), in the precise distance necessary to cast the long shadows that reach from tower to tower on the summer solstice. On June 21, a day known to Freemasons as St. John's Day, the shadow hypotenuse at 66.6 feet joins the upper window of one tower with the lower window of the opposite tower.

In the 56-36-66.6 triangle, one can immediately recognize 56 as a Masonic number, but what of 36 and 66.6? In Christianity the number 666 is the number of the beast, the anti-Christ: "this calls for wisdom— let anyone with understanding calculate the number of the beast for it is the number of man. Its number is 666." (Revelation 13:18) But in Masonic lore and Hebrew scripture the number 666 refers to Solomon's wealth and the number of gold bars used to build the temple. It is not

FIGURE 31—Summer Solstice Triangle, the Stonehenge of Knox. Collection of the author.

diabolic or ominous; on the contrary, it is a positive divine signifier. This meaning is referred to in 1 Kings 10:24 and 2 Chronicles 9:13: "Now the weight of gold that came to Solomon in one year was six hundred threescore and six talents of gold." Gold is the color of the sun, and the association of the sun with 666 and with Solomon's Temple became a recurrent theme in kabbalah and in occult philosophy. In 1509 the Renaissance magus-philosopher Cornelius Agrippa published and circulated *De Occulta Philosophia*, an encyclopedia and manual of occult practices.[22] It was translated into English, French, and German and was widely circulated. Ithiel Town had a copy in his library. Exploiting the connections between the color of gold, the sun, and the reference to the number 666, Agrippa identified the number 666 with the magic squares of the sun. Agrippa's reasoning is strictly astrological. The zodiac is divided into 12 houses, and each house has 30 degrees subdivided into three ten-degree decans. The whole therefore has 36 decans, and the sum of the integers 1 through 36 equals 666. In occult lore, when a six-by-six square is inscribed with the numbers 1 through 36 in a secret order, the result is a sun talisman or charm that will draw down God's creative and protective energy. Agrippa gave instructions for making sun squares, and esoteric geometers soon worked out the 56-36-66.6 triangle as a talismanic figure or charm capable of receiving the sun's generative power. The magical numbers 36 and 666 are "good" numbers because they hold the key to infusing earthly objects with a divine aura that will drive out darkness and evil. Ithiel Town may have understood how to make sun squares and triangles with the dimensions 56, 36, and 66.6, and he may have shared this knowledge with his apprentices and draftsmen. These inner secrets that combine esoteric geometry with occult philosophy would not have been widely shared and almost certainly were not recorded in writings that the public might see.

In occult philosophy the numbers 36 and 666 intersect the Masonic series 14, 28, 56, 112, 224 at the number 56. A triangle with a base of 36 and a hypotenuse of 66.6 will have a height of 56, and 56 was one Ulricson's favorite numbers. Old Main's upper tower windows at 56 feet aligned with the now missing corner towers, which were also at 56 feet. The tallest towers at 66 feet were the four towers flanking the entrances. The choice of 66 feet again seems to be a reference to Solomon's golden number. In the 1890s, the decision to install a hip roof and cover the platform led to the removal of the corner towers and also lowered the height of the tall towers to 60 feet, which is their current height. Regrettably, one cannot determine if the true height of the tall towers was 66 feet or 66.6 feet. But the position of the tower windows is unchanged, and on the summer solstice a shadow hypotenuse forms at 66.6 feet. The Masonic and occult sun numbers, 36, 56, and 66.6 are cleverly worked into the south and north facades, waiting for the summer solstice to make their triangular relationship visible to everyone. Another interpretation, which is more speculative and fanciful, holds that the magic triangle awaits the summer solstice to receive the sun and allow the divine energy that will flow from tower to tower and throughout the sacred network that surrounds the building. Like a highly geometric Stonehenge, Knox's Old Main greets the summer solstice with a once a year bridge of sun and shadow. In occult philosophy the sun represents God. The symbolic connections between God, the color gold, the sun, and the numbers 36, 56, and 666 were multiple ways of invoking spiritual communication between earthly objects and the divine source of life. The sun governs the zodiac, the planets, and human lives. It is the cosmic analog of the all seeing eye of providence, so prominent on the one-dollar bill and so pervasive in the art and architecture of Freemasonry. It may be mere coincidence that on St. John's Day a 36-56-66.6 sun triangle appears on the south side of Knox's Old Main, or it may have been a well thought out expression of Ulricson's belief that the sun will replenish the network of sacred geometry with divine energy. In this reading Ulricson worked out his tower and window placements to be sun receptacles. The towers collect the divine power, fill the tower cavities, and disperse its creative protective force throughout the network of sacred geometry. Thus the summer solstice renews the Chapel in the Sky each year with God's protective energy and goodness. This reasoning explains why the towers are situated as they are.

For a Swede who could remember the solstice sun holiday in Sweden, a sun talisman in Galesburg, Illinois, would make perfect sense. It recalled a holiday welcomed with riotous exuberance and enjoyed as a time of benevolent reverie and healthy optimism. In addition, in the Masonic tradition St. John's Day is the proper day to set cornerstones and consecrate buildings. Perhaps Ulricson sought to rectify the missing cornerstone ceremony by replacing it with the annual solar renewal of the sun triangle. Since explicit statements about Ulricson's plan are lacking, the ideas of a solar renewal or a repeatable consecration are conjectures. The evidence is circumstantial with principal support coming from the dimensions of Old Main, the placement of the windows, and the unquestionable appearance of the annual hypotenuse. Further, making a sun talisman is a spiritual correlate of the Daviséan aesthetic, which repeatedly and self-consciously draws attention to shadows connecting geometric points on a building. Uniting the two ideas may have been one of Ulricson's most creative insights.

From an artistic point of view, the placement of towers, windows, and porches indicates that Ulricson found an exceedingly brilliant way to express Davis's teachings on the interconnections of geometry, light, and shadow. The shadows move across the facade and heighten its already legible geometry. The sun becomes a tool or pointer to intensify the vertical and horizontal elements in the facades. The legible geometry springs to life in the sunlight and then falls into shadow as the day recedes. The entire display can be enjoyed without any reference to geometry or occult philosophy.

Today architecture is largely a mechanical profession governed by technical rationality, utilitarian goals, and advanced technology. A modern building serves the needs of its owners and users first. Its design and execution are controlled by the purely practical requirements. All is shaped by the prevailing technology. Everything must be fashionable and efficient. As the fireproof iron box in Knoxville Hall of

Records proves, Ulricson knew how to meet utilitarian goals; however, Old Main and Augustana Church show that he could pursue aesthetic and religious aims reaching beyond practical necessity.

Today the religious and moral convictions of the builder are virtually never a part of the design equation, though those of the clients may be included. The aesthetic preferences of architects are extremely important, and they cannot be separated from the work at hand; however, their spiritual and religious convictions are generally excluded. They find no conscious expression in the edifice. Devoid of any transcendent meaning, the modern building is liberated from all mythology and narrative. Its various rooms and chambers may house or showcase artifacts that have symbolic meaning, but the building itself is no such thing. A structure succeeds if it is efficient, functional, technologically sophisticated, and trendsetting. By contrast Ulricson—and earlier, Town and Davis—strove to create buildings that expressed transcendent meanings in symbols, special numbers, proportions, and iconography. They included their religious, spiritual, and philosophical beliefs in their work, albeit in cleverly disguised ways. They believed esoteric geometry was the key to making a beautiful edifice with divine protection and sanction. The mystic ratios and sacred numbers were both the means and the aim of good design. In Anti-Masonic America, alchemical architects could not broadcast their beliefs about sacred geometry, the power of philosopher's stones, and the Divine Architect and Geometer of the Universe. They could translate their convictions into bricks and stone but not into words and books. It is possible that Ulricson worked out his elaborate designs of interlocking geometry and privileged ratios as an exercise of craft and skill and nothing more. In this view he was more like a modern architect employing the tools he knew best, which happened to be esoteric geometry. His tool kit contained the well-understood formulae of the golden ratio and a Masonic number series. He used them not as ends expressing meaning but as a means to produce an attractive building. The Greek, Gothic, and Tuscan style revivals were Ulricson's instruments for exercising his talent. His knowledge of the Town and Davis portfolios gave him the pieces and the plans that he needed to be a professional architect, not just a glorified builder. Blanchard, the Knox trustees, and the Lutherans in Andover gave him the opportunity to build big, and he executed what he knew best. He made artful choices guided by practice and private knowledge but without the convictions of a believer.

The reasoning in this investigation relied heavily on the hypothesis that Ulricson's repeated and rigorous applications of esoteric geometry went beyond instrumental thinking. Ulricson could have avoided the risky and controversial alchemical themes and all Masonic symbolism, as he did in his Tuscan style buildings. He had other tools and plans that would have immunized him from all possibility of detection. He could have avoided all risk by simply making slight alterations in the dimensions of his buildings, but he didn't. His rigor speaks the language of conviction. When conceiving of Old Main with its chapel and Augustana with its great nave and tower, Ulricson drew deeply from the well of esoteric philosophy. From opening day onward Old Main and Augustana Church puzzled observers. No one knew for certain what to call their styles of architecture. Augustana looked somewhat like churches in Sweden but not entirely. Old Main looked like Collegiate Gothic, but it was also different in some inexplicable way. These puzzles in observation and in classification stem from the deeper themes found in esoteric geometry, talismanic building, and the union of architecture with the occult. Old Main has a philosopher's stone to reconcile opposites, and that makes all the difference in understanding its place in architectural history and in determining the intentions of its architect. Ulricson's buildings retained their hidden meanings for a century and a half. While more is known about them now, not everything is revealed. There remains a pendulum of uncertainty in the Ulricson story swinging between the clever professional who made artful choices and the true believer who worked from conviction. The cultic Ulricson and the practical Ulricson coexist, like the Greek-Gothic synthesis in Knox's Old Main. Being deprived of definitive answers in no way diminishes the aesthetic pleasure of enjoying Ulricson's masterpieces. On the contrary, their newly discovered connections with Town and Davis, the Jacksonian era, Freemasonry, and esoteric geometry make them even greater treasures.

Notes

1 — A SURPRISING IRONY

1. Ernest Olson, *The Swedish Element in Illinois, A Survey of the Past Seven Decades* (Chicago: Swedish-American Biographical Association, 1917), 31.

2. Jane B. Davies, comp. "Works and Projects, 1803–1892" in Amelia Peck (ed.), *Alexander Jackson Davis: American Architect, 1803–1892* (New York: Rizzoli and Metropolitan Museum of Art, 1992), 108.

3. Davies, "Works and Projects," 109, 119. Talbot Hamlin, *Greek Revival Architecture in America: being an account of important trends in American architecture and American life prior to the war between the states* (New York: Oxford University Press, 1944; Dover Books Reprint, 1964), 310. Hamlin states, "*The WPA Guide to Illinois,* a publication of the Federal Writers' Project, credits the Illinois capitol to John Francis Rague, the architect of the Iowa capitol. Rague may have acted as superintendent, but Town and Davis were undoubtedly the designing architects." For a different view, see Wayne C. Temple and Sunderine Temple, *Abraham Lincoln and Illinois' Fifth Capitol* (Mahomet, IL: Mayhaven Pub., 1988).

4. Alan B. Solomon, "The Reconstruction of the Ground Zero Area and The Rescue of the Facade of 211 Pearl Street, Unearthing the Esoteric Interests of Architect Ithiel Town and the Owner William Colgate" in *Masonic and Esoteric Heritage. A New Perspective for Art and Conservation Policies* (Den Haag, Netherlands: Stichting OVN, 2005), 112. Also, Burkhard Bilger, "Mystery On Pearl Street," *The New Yorker.* (January 1, 2008), 56–68.

5. Lydia Sigourney, "The Residence and Library of Ithiel Town, Esq.," in *The Ladies Companion, a Monthly Magazine.* 1st Series, 10 No. 1 (1839), 123.

6. Town owned copies of Francis Barrett's *The Magus; or, Celestial intelligencer, being a complete system of occult philosophy. . .* (London: Lackington, Allen, 1801) and *The Golden Fleece—containing The Mirror of Alchemy* (London: Prometheus Press, 2005).

7. Thomas Taylor, *The Theoretic Arithmetic of the Pythagoreans.* (London: Prometheus Press Reprints, 2006), 10.

8. Ithiel Town, "The Mathematical Exercises of Ithiel Town (1823–1840)," Town Collection in the Beinecke Rare Book and Manuscript Library, Yale University, New Haven, CT. For a description of Town's studio and his draftsmen, see Chapter 5 in John Donoghue, *Alexander Jackson Davis, Romantic Architect 1803–1892* (New York: Arno Press, 1982), no page numbers.

9. Solomon, 111.

10. The temple, built by Hugh Reingle, opened on the traditional day of consecration, the summer solstice, or St. John's Day, June 21, 1824. "First

Masonic Temple File," Masonic Archives, Livingston Masonic Archives, New York City.

11. G. Everett Arden, *Augustana Heritage: A History of the Augustana Lutheran Church* (Rock Island, IL: Augustana Press, 1963), 149.

12. Jonathan Blanchard, "My Life Work" (unpublished autobiographical statement typescript). Blanchard File, Knox College Archives (hereafter KCA), 5.

13. Donoghue, "Architectural Innovations of Town and Davis," in *Alexander Jackson Davis, Romantic Architect,* Chapter Five, no page numbers.

2 — THE URBANE MR. ULRICSON

1. *Knox College Expense Book,* 1857, KCA.

2. *Knox College Catalogue,* 1855, KCA.

3. Hartneck Interview, Architect File, KCA.

4. Executive Committee Minutes, June 1856, KCA.

5. *Knox College Expense Book,* 1856, KCA.

6. Timothy Hartnek Papers, Ulricson Family Interview, Peoria Historical Society, Bradley University Special Collections, Peoria, Illinois.

7. Hartneck Interview, Architect File, KCA.

8. Ibid.

9. Alex G. Davidson, "The Swedish Constitution," <www freemasons. com/Swedish constitution> (accessed 2007). Also "Swedish Order of Freemasons," <www.frimurarorden.se/eng/> (accessed 2007).

10. Oscar Ulricson note cards, Architect File, KCA.

11. Nils William Olsson, *Swedish Passenger Arrivals in New York 1820–1830* (Chicago: Swedish Pioneer Historical Society: 1967), 20–25. Also, Henry C. Whyman, *The Hedstroms and the Bethel Ship Saga: Methodist Influence on Swedish Life* (Edwardsville, Illinois: Southern Illinois University Press, 1992), 85.

12. Philip Hone, *The Diary of Philip Hone,* 2 Vols. Alan Nevins, ed. (New York: Dodd, Mead, 1927), Vol. 1, 245, entry for Monday, March 6, 1837.

13. "Frances Ulricson Statement," Architect File, KCA.

14. Hamlin, 140. Also see James Gallier, *Autobiography of James Gallier* (Reading, MA: DeCapo Press, 1972). Reprint of the 1864 edition.

15. Hamlin, 141.

16. A close examination of the list of architects practicing in New York City as found in Dennis Steadman Francis (compiler), *Architects in Practice in New York City—1840–1900.* New York: The Committee for the Preservation of Architectural Records, 1979, confirms that Fredric Diaper, a young man of 28, did not open his office until 1838.

17. *New York Daily Express,* February 14, 1840, preserved in A.J. Davis, "Letter Book," Series I, Davis Manuscript Collection, New York Public Library.

18. *United State Census of 1850*. Washington, D.C. 1853.

19. "Oscar Ulricson's note cards," Architect File, KCA.

20. Benjamin Cowell, *Story of St. Paul's Parish* (Peoria, IL: Bourland Press, 1926), 21. Peoria Historical Society Archives, Bradley University Library, Peoria, IL.

21. Cowell, 42–44.

22. Ibid., 46.

23. Emmet E. Eklund, *His Name was Jonas: A Biography of Jonas Swensson* (Rock Island, IL: Augustana Historical Society, 1988), 71–72.

24. Albert G. Mackey, s.v. "Urn" in *A Lexicon of Freemasonry* (Reprint edition. New York: Barnes and Noble, 2004), 508.

25. "Swensson-Ulricson Correspondence," Swensson Collection, Evangelical Lutheran Church in America Archives, Elk Grove, Illinois.

3 — FREEMASONS AND ANTI-MASONS

1. *Galesburg Free Democrat,* July 6, 1857.

2. *Galesburg Free Democrat,* July 2, 1857. The protest coincided with a meeting of the Knox Alumni Association. Both groups supported Blanchard.

3. "Trustee Minutes," June 1857, KCA.

4. *Galesburg Free Democrat,* August 25, 1857.

5. Charles Ulricson, "Architect's Specifications for Main College," Vault File, KCA.

6. Mary Ann Clawson, *Constructing Brotherhood: Class, Gender, and Fraternalism* (Princeton, NJ: Princeton University Press, 1989), 145–47.

7. George Washington's letter to Massachusetts Grand Lodge of Masons, December 27, 1792, reprinted in *A Treasury of Masonic Thought,* Carl Glick, ed. (New York: Vail-Ballou Press, Inc., 1959), 204.

8. C.E. Hovey, "Knox College," *The Illinois Teacher,* Vol. 3, 1857 392.

9. Jonathan Blanchard, *Standard Freemasonry Illustrated* (Chicago: Ezra Cook & Co. 1912; reprinted by Kessinger Publishing, 2008), 19. Also, "Freemasonry and Civil Government," address given September 10, 1888, Blanchard File, KCA.

10. William Preston Vaughn, *The Anti-Masonic Party* (Lexington: University of Kentucky Press, 1983), 52.

11. Hiram Ferris was not related to the Knox trustee Sylvanus Ferris.

12. Joel E. Ferris, "Hiram Gano Ferris of Illinois and California," in *California Historical Society Quarterly,* Vol. 26, No. 4, December 1947, 291.

13. The practice seems to have stopped after 1850.

14. Hermann Muelder, *Fighters for Freedom: The History of Anti-slavery Activities of Men and Women Associated with Knox College* (New York: Columbia University Press, 1959), 236. In 1855 Beta Theta Pi had been secretly established.

Muelder described Blanchard's effect on secret clubs at the college, 349.

15. Blanchard File, KCA.

16. [Anon.] "Smoke," in *Knoxiana* and *Oak Leaf: 1856–1857* (Galesburg, IL: Knox College and Sherman Book Printer, 1857), 251.

17. *Galesburg City Directory, 1856.* Everett R. Turnbull, *The Rise and Progress of Freemasonry in Illinois 1783–1952* (Springfield: Grand Lodge of Illinois, 1952), 154.

18. Vaughn, 169.

19. C. E. Bryant, "The Student's Farewell," (private printing, Galesburg, 1857) KCA, 20.

20. Hermann Muelder, *Missionaries and Muckrakers: The First Hundred Years of Knox College.* (Urbana: University of Illinois Press, 1984), 236.

21. Alan B. Solomon, "The Reconstruction of the Ground Zero Area and the Rescue of the Facade of 211 Pearl Street. Unearthing the Esoteric Interests of the Architect Ithiel Town and the Owner William Colgate," in *Masonic and Esoteric Heritage. A New Perspective for Art and Conservation Policies* (Den Haag, Netherlands: Stichting OVN, 2005), 111.

22. Hamlin, xvii.

4 — MAN OF THE HOUR

1. "Trustee's Minutes," December 25, 1855, KCA.

2. A.J. Davis was the first to use the name "Collegiate Gothic" in 1834. See Paul Venable Turner, *Campus: An American Planning Tradition* (New York: Architectural History Foundation; Cambridge, MA: MIT Press, 1984), 124.

3. P. Atkinson, "How Strangers See Us," *Bloomington Pantograph,* Sept. 16, 1855, 5–8

4. "Knox Trustee Minutes," June 1856, KCA.

5. Bryant, "The Student's Farewell," 12.

6. Ibid., 14.

7. Ernest E. Calkins, *They Broke the Prairie: Being Some Account of the Settlement of the Upper Mississippi Valley by Religious and Educational Pioneers, Told in Terms of One City, Galesburg, and One College, Knox.* (Urbana: University of Illinois Press, 1989, reissued with an introduction by Rodney O. Davis, 1989. First published for the Galesburg Centenary, New York: Scribner's, 1937), 261.

8. Ibid., 141–44.

9. Address before Knox County Historical Society by Erastus S. Wilcox (1906), reported in Calkins, 139.

10. Border image from "Map of Galesburg 1855," prepared by N. Losey, KCA.

11. James Early, "The Romantic Revivals: History and Association" in *Romanticism and American Architecture* (New York: A.S. Barnes and Company, 1965), 21–50.

12. "Trustees' Report," June 25, 1856, KCA.

13. "Trustees' Minutes," December 25, 1855, KCA.

14. *Galesburg Free Democrat* and *Peoria Spectator,* from Jan.–Aug. 1857. Also, *Peoria Weekly Republican,* May 2, 1856: "Mr. Ulricson will receive $90,000 to complete Main College and the Female College."

15. "Trustees' Report," June 15, 1857, KCA.

16. Glen Patton, "Chapel in the Sky," *Architectural Review* (March 1969), 177.

17. *The New American,* May 27, 1837, quoted in LeRoy E. Kimball, "The Old University Building and the Society's Years on Washington Square," *New York Historical Society Quarterly* (July 1948), 158.

18. Patton, 21.

19. "Trustees' Minutes," December 25, 1855, KCA.

20. Patton, 178.

5 — THE PHILOSOPHER'S STONE

1. Mackey, s.v. "Pythagoras," *A Lexicon of Freemasonry,* 387.

2. Mackey, s.v. "Square," *A Lexicon of Freemasonry,* 450.

3. Thomas Taylor "Introduction" in *Philosophical and Mathematical Commentaries of Proclus on the First Book of Euclid's Elements.* Translated by Thomas Taylor (London: Prometheus Trust Press, 2006; reprint of edition by Payne and Egerton, London: 1792), 30–31. Also, for the origin of the unity figure known as a dodekatopos, see "Horoscopes and Prognostications" in Matilde Battistini, *Astrology, Magic, and Alchemy in Art.* Translated by Rosanna M. Giammanco Frongia (Los Angeles: J. Paul Getty Museum, 2007), 100.

4. "Hartneck Interview," Architect File, KCA.

5. "Pearl Street Revival," <http://pearlstreetrevival.typepad.com> (accessed 2008) and Arthur Scully, *James Dakin, Architect: His Career in New York and the South (*Baton Rouge: Louisiana State University Press, 1973), 19, 137. Dakin was a Royal Arch Mason and a member of St. James Masonic Lodge in Baton Rouge.

6. Frank Albo, "Masonic Parlante in a Canadian Temple of Democracy: The Manitoba Legislative Building as Initiatory Theatre," in *The Hermetic Code: Unlocking One of Manitoba's Greatest Secrets* (Winnipeg: Winnipeg Free Press: 2007).

7. Robert Lomas, "The Cross, the *Vesica Piscis* and Masonic Astrology," in *The Secrets of Freemasonry: Revealing the Suppressed Tradition* (London: Magpie Books, 2006), 206–9. Also, J.S.M. Ward, "The Vesica Piscis," in *Freemasonry and the Ancient Gods* (London: Simpkin, Marshall, Hamilton, Kent & Co. Ltd., 1921).

8. "Note from Clarkson Family," Architect File, KCA.

9. Janet Grieg Post, *Knox Alumnus Supplement* (Summer, 1937), 68.

10. Steven C. Bullock, *Revolutionary Brotherhood: Freemasonry and the Transformation of the American Social Order, 1730–1840* (Chapel Hill: University of North Carolina Press, 1996), 16.

11. *Galesburg Free Democrat,* July 3, 1856, "The foundation for the main bldg. of Knox College is nearly completed. The o ... [sic] is large cut stone and presents a beautiful as well as a massive appearance."

12. "Free and speculative masonry is but an application of the art of operative masonry to moral and intellectual purposes. Our ancestors worked at the construction of the Temple of Jerusalem; while we are engaged in the erection of a more immortal edifice—the temple of the mind. They employed their implements for merely mechanical purposes, but we use them symbolically, with more exalted designs." Mackey, *A Lexicon of Freemasonry,* 520.

13. Mackey, s.v. "Trestle Board," *A Lexicon of Freemasonry,* 498.

14. Interviews with Merle Banks and Martin Reichel, June 2006, Galesburg, IL.

6—THE SACRED GEOMETRY

1. *Peoria Daily Spectator,* August 5, 1857.

2. C.E. Hovey, "Knox College," *The Illinois Teacher*, Vol. 3, 1857, 385–93.

3. Hovey, 388.

4. Luca Pacioli, *De Divine Proportione*, 1509 (Ambrosiana fascimile reproduction, 1956; Silvana fascimile reproduction, 1982). Robert Lawlor, *Sacred Geometry: Philosophy and Practice* (New York: Crossroad, 1982). Mario Livio, *The Golden Ratio: The Story of Phi, the World's Most Astonishing Number* (New York: Broadway Books, 2002). Livio quotes Johannes Kepler (1571–1630), "Geometry has two great treasures: one is the theorem of Pythagoras, the other the division of a line into mean and extreme portions," 62. Rochelle Newman and Martha Boles, *The Golden Relationship: Art, Math & Nature.* Vol. 1 (Second Edition) (Bradford, MA: Pythagorean Press, 1992), 32–46.

5. Other examples of Blanchard's identification of Freemasonry with Satanism: "Freemasonry and the Bible give opposite answers to the question of salvation, . . . the one, . . . promises salvation by ceremonies, which in effect is salvation by Satan; the other by Christ." Jonathan Blanchard, *Standard Freemasonry Illustrated* (Chicago: Ezra Cook & Co. 1912), reprinted by Kessinger Publishing Co. 2003, 19. "The great power of the lodge, as of all false religious, is in its worship. The devil is its god, whom the Bible calls a serpent, and he charms men, as literal snakes charm their victims, and then swallows them." "Freemasonry and Civil Government," address given October 9, 1888, Blanchard File, KCA.

6. Alexander Jackson Davis, "Apollo Lectures," Manuscript Collection, Journal Series I, New York Public Library, 229.

7. The hooded moldings and the trim lines demarcate the proportions as calculated by counting courses of block: AD/AB = π, AD/AC = $\sqrt{2}$, AF/AC = 2, AF/AD = $1/\phi$ =.618, AE/AF = $\sqrt{3}$.

8. BE/AB =32´/20´, AD/EF= 47´/29´, AD/AC = 47´/29´.

7—A QUESTION OF STYLE

1. Calder Loth and Julius T. Sadler Jr., *The Only Proper Style: Gothic Architecture in America* (Boston: New York Graphic Society, 1975), 91.

2. Nora Pat Small, "A Building for the Ages: The History and Architecture of Old Main" (Eastern Illinois University)," <http://www.eid.edu/laclite/coles> (accessed September 2008), 1.

3. Richard P. Dober, *Old Main: Fame, Fate and Contributions to Campus Planning and Design* (Ann Arbor: Society of College and University Planning, 2007).

4. Knox County Courthouse, designed by John Mandeville of Bergen, New Jersey, in 1837. Mandeville lived in Knoxville and personally supervised construction of his prostyle temple with four Doric columns.

5. James Stuart and Nicholas Revett, *The Antiquities of Athens and Other Monuments of Greece* (London: Charles Tilt, 1792; reprinted by Elibron Replica Classics, 2005), Vol 1. 12–22.

6. Hamlin, 339.

7. "Davis Journal," I:42, Davis Manuscript Collection, New York Public Library.

8. Philip A. Bruce, *History of the University of Virginia, 1819–1919* (New York: Macmillan,1922), Vol. 1 1:189–90.

9. Rudolf Wittkower, *Architectural Principles in the Age of Humanism* (New York: Norton, 1962), 76–82.

10. Fredrick D. Nichols, *Palladio in America* (New York: Rizzoli, 1978), 111–25.

11. Roger Hale Newton, *Town and Davis, Architects* (New York: Columbia University Press, 1942), 105.

12. Susanne Brendel-Pandich, "From Cottage to Castles: The Country House Designs of Alexander Jackson Davis," *Alexander Jackson Davis, American Architect, 1803–1892,* edited by Amelia Peck (New York: Rizzoli and Metropolitan Museum of Art, 1992), 59.

13. Jane B. Davies, "Alexander J. Davis, Creative American Architect," *Alexander Jackson Davis, American Architect, 1803–1892,* edited by Amelia Peck (New York: Rizzoli and Metropolitan Museum of Art, 1992), 10.

14. Amelia Peck, s.v. "Alexander Jackson Davis (1803–1892)," *The Metropolitan Museum of Art Presents a Timeline of Art History* (New York: The Metropolitan Museum of Art, 2000), <http://www.metmuseum.org/toah> (accessed October 2004).

15. A.J. Davis, "Diary," also known as "Letter Book," Series I, Davis Manuscript Collection, New York Public Library, 545–50.

16. Ibid., 546.

17. Ibid., 547.

18. A.J. Davis, "Diary," Series I, Davis Manuscript Collection, New York Public Library, 183.

19. Theodore F. Jones, *New York University, 1833–1932* (New York: New York University Press, 1933), 43.

20. Donoghue, *Alexander Jackson Davis, Romantic Architect, 1803-1892,* Chapter III, footnote 45, no pagination. Also, Thomas Aldrich Bailey, "Among the Studios," *Our Young Folks,* July–Sept. 1866, 343.

21. *Galesburg Free Democrat* and *Peoria Spectator,* Jan.–Aug. 1857.

22. *Peoria Spectator,* March 18, 1857.

23. *The Knox Student,* October 19, 1933.

24. *Galesburg Register-Mail,* February 21, 1933.

25. Gwen Luxow, "Old Main and the Knox Idea," (Knox College, Senior Honors Thesis, 1990), directed by Dr. John Strassburger. KCA.

26. "In 1920, Henry M. Seymour promised the Trustees a library building and personally made good on the pledge. He selected the architects Coolidge and Hodgdon of Chicago, and personally provided the handsome cream-colored limestone from a quarry on his farm in Payson, Adams County, Illinois. The building was dedicated on Founders Day, 1928." <http:library.knox. edu> (accessed October 2007).

27. "Old Main Series," Correspondence File, Letter of April 27, 1927. KCA. McClelland photographed the interior prior to demolition and thus preserved the only record of the rooms before renovation.

28. *Knox Alumnus Supplement,* 1937, 66.

29. "Old Main Series," Correspondence File, KCA.

30. "Remarks—Commencement June 15, 1937," Janet Grieg Post File, KCA.

8—THE LIGHT IN JUNE

1. Bray Hammond, *Banks and Politics in America, from the Revolution to the Civil War* (Princeton: Princeton University Press, 1957), 710.

2. *Galesburg Free Democrat,* August 28, 1857.

3. "Executive Committee Minutes," March and October 1858, KCA.

4. "O.H. Browning to President Lincoln, Wed. July 04, 1860," Abraham Lincoln Papers, Library of Congress (Electronic Edition), Series I, General Correspondence.

5. Hermann R. Muelder, *Missionaries and Muckrakers: The First Hundred Years of Knox College* (Urbana: University of Illinois Press, 1984), 33.

6. Muelder, 37.

7. Ella F. Arnold, "Interview," *The Knox Alumnus,* March 1927.

8. "Executive Committee Minutes," October 1867, KCA.

9. "Trouble at Knox College," *The Monmouth Courier,* March 1868. Also *Knox College Catalogue,* 1867–1868, 18.

10. Paul R. Anderson, *Platonism in the Midwest* (New York: Temple University Publications, 1963), 28–69.

11. "Executive Committee Minutes," May 10, 1869, KCA.

12. "Executive Committee Minutes," September 5, 1868, KCA.

13. Jonathan Blanchard, "My Life Work," unpublished autobiography, KCA.

14. [Anon,] "Smoke," *Knoxiana* and *Oak Leaf:* 1857, 251–53.

15. "Ulricson Obituary," Architect File, KCA.

16. Amelia Peck, ed. *Alexander Jackson Davis, American Architect, 1803–1892* (New York: Rizzoli and Metropolitan Museum of Art, 1992), 10.

17. Quoted in Francis R. Kowsky, "Simplicity and Dignity: The Public and Institutional Buildings of Alexander Jackson Davis," in *Alexander Jackson Davis, American Architect, 1803–1892,* edited by Amelia Peck (New York: Rizzoli and Metropolitan Museum of Art, 1992), 47.

18. [Anon.] *History of Augustana Evangelical Lutheran Church* (Andover, IL, 150th Anniversary Report), 5.

19. Mackey, s.v. "Point within a Circle," *A Lexicon of Freemasonry,* 362.

20. Mackey, s.v. "Rule," *A Lexicon of Freemasonry,* 421.

21. Conrad Bergendoff (editor and translator), "Letters from Andover to Hogarp, Sweden (1858–1898)," Augustana College Occasional Paper No. 17, 1988.

22. Cornelius Agrippa, Book II: 22, *Three Books of Occult Philosophy (1533),* edited and translated by Donald Tyson (St Paul: Llewellyn Publications, 1993), 319–20.

.

Bibliography

MANUSCRIPT COLLECTIONS

Augustana Lutheran Church Collections:
Evangelical Lutheran Church in America, Elk Grove Village, IL.
Swenson Immigration Center, Augustana College, Rock Island, IL.
Davis Collections:
Avery Architectural Library, Columbia University, New York, NY.
Metropolitan Museum of Art (Print Room), New York, NY.
New York Historical Society, New York, NY.
New York Public Library (Manuscript Room)
University of North Carolina (University Archives, Electronic Edition), Chapel
    Hill, NC.
Masonic Collections:
Livingston Masonic Library, Periodicals Collection, New York, NY.
Iowa Masonic Library, Cedar Rapids, IA.
Town Collections:
Town Papers, New Haven Colony Historical Society, New Haven, CT.
Town Papers, Beirnecke Rare Book Collection, Yale University, New Haven, CT.
Ulricson Collections:
Peoria Historical Society, Bradley University Special Collections, Peoria, IL.
Knox College Archives, Knox College, Galesburg, IL.

PUBLISHED MATERIAL

Adams, Wayne. *Architecture, Ambition and Americans: A Social History of American
    Architecture*. New York: Free Press of Glencoe, 1964.
Agrippa, Cornelius, *Three Books of Occult Philosophy (1533)*. Edited and trans-
    lated by Donald Tyson. St Paul: Llewellyn Publications, 1993.
Albo, Frank. *The Hermetic Code: Unlocking One of Manitoba's Greatest Secrets*. Win-
    nipeg: Winnipeg Free Press, 2006.
Anderson, Paul R. *Platonism in the Midwest*. New York: Temple University Pub-
    lications, 1963.
Andrist, Ralph K. ed. *George Washington: A Biography in His Own Words*. New
    York: Harper and Row, 1972.
Anonymous. *Manual of Work*. Grand Lodge of Virginia: A.F. & A.M. Richmond,
    1986.
———. "Swedish Order of Freemasons." <www.frimurarorden.se/eng/> Accessed 2007.

————. *History of Augustana Evangelical Lutheran Church.* Andover, IL. 150th Anniversary Report.

Arden, G. Everett. *Augustana Heritage, A History of Augustana Lutheran Church.* Rock Island, IL: Augustana Press, 1963.

Atkinson, P. "How Strangers See Us." *Bloomington Pantograph.* Sept. 16, 1855, 5.

Bailey, Thomas Aldrich. "Among the Studios." *Our Young Folks,* July–Sept. 1866, 341–357.

Barrett, Francis. *The Magus; or, Celestial intelligencer, being a complete system of occult philosophy. . .* London: Lackington, Allen, 1801. Reprinted as *Celestial Intelligencer, A System of Occult Philosophy, Natural Magic, Alchemy, & Talismanic Magic & The Philosopher's Stone Made Visible.* Reprint edition. Portland, OR: None Such, 2007.

————. *The Golden Fleece—containing The Mirror of Alchemy.* London: Prometheus Press, 2005 (Reprint of the 1792 edition).

Battistini, Matilde. *Astrology, Magic, and Alchemy in Art.* Translated by Rosanna M. Giammanco Frongia. Los Angeles: J. Paul Getty Museum, 2007.

Bergendoff, Conrad. (editor and translator). "Letters from Andover to Hogarp, Sweden (1858–1898)." Augustana College Occasional Paper No. 17, 1988.

Bilger, Burkhard. "Mystery On Pearl Street." *The New Yorker.* January 1, 2007, 56–68.

Blanchard, Jonathan. "Introduction." In *Standard Freemasonry Illustrated.* Chicago: Ezra Cook & Co. 1912. Reprinted by Kessinger Publishers, 2008.

————. "My Life Work," unpublished autobiographical statement, Blanchard File, Knox College Archives.

Blanchard, Jonathan, David MacDill, and Edward Beecher. *Secret Societies: A Discussion of Their Character and Claims* (1867). Reprinted by Kessinger Publishers, 2008.

Brendel-Pandich, Susanne. "From Cottage to Castles: The Country House Designs of Alexander Jackson Davis." In *Alexander Jackson Davis: American Architect, 1803–1892.* Edited by Amelia Peck. New York: Rizzoli and Metropolitan Museum of Art, 1992, 58–88.

Brown, William Moseley. *George Washington, Freemason.* Richmond: Garrett and Massie, 1952.

Bruce, Philip A. *History of the University of Virginia, 1819–1919, 5 vols.* New York: Macmillan, 1922.

Bryant, C.E. "The Student's Farewell." Knox College, Galesburg, IL: Sherman Book Printer, 1857: 15–32.

————. "Knox College &c." *Knoxiana* and *Oak Leaf.* Knox College, Galesburg, IL: Sherman Book Printer, 1857: 11–15.

Bullock, Steven C. *Revolutionary Brotherhood: Freemasonry and the Transformation of the American Social Order, 1730–1840.* Chapel Hill: University of North Carolina Press, 1996.

Calkins, Ernest E. *They Broke the Prairie: Being Some Account of the Settlement of the Upper Mississippi Valley by Religious and Educational Pioneers, Told in Terms of One City, Galesburg, and One College, Knox.* Urbana: University of Illinois Press, 1989, reissued with an introduction by Rodney O. Davis, 1989. First published for the Galesburg Centenary, New York: Scribner's, 1937.

California Historical Society Quarterly, San Francisco: 1947.

Callahan, Charles H. *Washington, The Man and the Mason.* Washington, D.C.: Press of Gibson Bros., 1913.

Cambridge Chronicle, 1867. Cambridge, IL.

Chan, Sewell. "Three Cryptic Shapes Pose a Puzzle." City Room Blog. *New York Times,* July 23, 2007. <http://cityroom.blogs.nytimes.com/2007/07/23/three-cryptic-shapes-pose-a-puzzle>

Clawson, Mary Ann. *Constructing Brotherhood: Class, Gender, and Fraternalism.* Princeton, NJ: Princeton University Press, 1989.

Cowell, Benjamin. *Story of St. Paul's Parish.* Peoria, IL: Bourland Press, 1926.

Curl, James Stevens. *The Art and Architecture of Freemasonry.* London: Batsford Press, 1991.

Davidson, Alex. "The Swedish Constitution." <www freemasons.com/Swedish-constitution>. Accessed 2007.

Davies, Jane B. *A.J. Davis and American Classicism: An Exhibition.* Tarrytown: Sleepy Hollow Press, 1989.

———. "Alexander J. Davis, Creative American Architect." *Alexander Jackson Davis, American Architect, 1803–1892.* Edited by Amelia Peck. New York: Rizzoli and Metropolitan Museum of Art, 1992, 8–22.

Dober, Richard P. *Old Main: Fame, Fate and Contributions to Campus Planning and Design.* Ann Arbor: Society of College and University Planning, 2007.

Doczi, György. *The Power of Limits: Proportional Harmonies in Nature, Art, and Architecture.* Boulder, CO: Shambala Press, 1994.

Donoghue, John. *Alexander Jackson Davis, Romantic Architect 1803–1892.* New York: Arnos Press, 1982.

Dumenil, Lynn. *Freemasonry and American Culture 1880–1930.* Princeton, NJ: Princeton University Press, 1984.

Dunlap, William. *History of the Rise and Progress of the Arts of Design in the United States.* New York: George Scott, 1834.

Early, James. *Romanticism and American Architecture.* New York: A.S. Barnes, 1965.

Eastlake, Charles. *A History of the Gothic Revival.* New York and Leicester: Humanities Press and Leicester University Press, 1970.

Eklund, Emmet E. *His Name was Jonas: A Biography of Jonas Swensson.* Rock Island, IL: Augustana Historical Society, 1988.

Fay, Theodore S. *Views in New-York and its environs from accurate, characteristic,*

& *picturesque drawings, taken on the spot, expressly for this work, by Dakin, architect; with historical, topographical, & critical illustrations by Theodore S. Fay; assisted by several distinguished literary gentlemen.* New York: Peabody & Co., 1831.

Ferris, Joel E. "Hiram Gano Ferris of Illinois and California." *California Historical Society Quarterly.* Vol. 26, No. 4, December 1947.

Francis, Dennis Steadman. *Architects in practice, New York City, 1840–1900.* New York: Committee for the Preservation of Architectural Records, 1980.

Galesburg City Directory, 1856. Galesburg, IL

Galesburg Free Democrat, 1855–1860. Galesburg, IL

Galesburg Register-Mail, 1937. Galesburg, IL

Gallier, James. *Autobiography of James Gallier, Architect.* Read, MA: DeCapo Press, 1972. (Reprint of the 1864 edition.)

Greenough, Horatio. *The Travels, Observations, and Experience of a Yankee Stonecutter.* New York: G.P. Putnam, 1852.

Glick, Carl (editor). *A Treasury of Masonic Thought.* New York: Vail-Ballou Press, Inc., 1959.

Goodman, Paul. *Towards a Christian Republic: Antimasonry and the Great Transition in New England, 1826–1836.* New York: Oxford University Press, 1988.

Hafertepe, Kenneth and James F. O'Gorman (editors). *American Architects and Their Books to 1848.* Amherst: University of Massachusetts Press, 2001.

Hall, Manly P. *An Encyclopedic Outline of Masonic, Hermetic, Quabbalistic and Rosicrucian Symbolical Philosophy; Being an Interpretation of the Secret Teachings Concealed within the Rituals, Allegories and Mysteries of All Ages.* San Francisco: H.S. Crocker Company, 1928.

Hambidge, Jay. *The Parthenon and Other Greek Temples; Their Dynamic Symmetry.* New Haven: Yale University Press 1924.

———. *The Elements of Dynamic Symmetry.* Reprint, New York: Dover, 1967.

Hamlin, Talbot. *Greek Revival Architecture in America: being an account of important trends in American architecture and American life prior to the war between the states . . .*New York: Oxford University Press, 1944; Reprint, New York: Dover Books, 1964.

Harwood, Jeremy. *The Freemasons.* London: Hermes House, 2006.

Hilton, Tim. *John Ruskin.* New Haven, CT: Yale University Press, 2002.

Hodapp, Christopher. *Freemasons for Dummies.* Hoboken, NJ: Wiley Publishing, 2005.

———. *Solomon's Builders: Freemasons, Founding Fathers and the Secrets of Washington, D.C.* Berkley: Ulysses Press, 2007.

Holt, Michael. *Political Parties and American Political Development: From the Age of Jackson to the Age of Lincoln.* Baton Rouge: Louisiana State University Press, 1992.

Hone, Philip. *The Diary of Philip Hone*. 2 vols. Edited and with an introduction by Allan Nevins. New York: Dodd and Mead, 1927.

Hovey, C.E. "Knox College." *The Illinois Teacher*. Vol. 3 (1857): 385–93.

Huntley, H.E. *The Divine Proportion: A Study in Mathematical Beauty*. New York: Dover Publications, 1970.

Huss, Wayne A. *The Master Builders: A History of the Grand Lodge of Free and Accepted Masons of Pennsylvania*. Philadelphia: Grand Lodge, 1989.

Illinois Teacher, 1857. Bloomington, IL.

Imbert, Anthony. Life in New York, Lithograph Series. *Views of the Public Buildings in New York*. New York: 1828.

Ivins, William M. *Art and Geometry; a Study in Space Intuitions*. New York: Dover Books, 1964.

Jones, Theodore F. *New York University, 1833–1932*. New York: New York University Press, 1933.

Kaufmann, Emil. *Architecture In The Age Of Reason; Baroque and Postbaroque in England, Italy, and France*. Cambridge: Harvard University Press, 1955.

Kimball, LeRoy E. "The Old University Building and the Society's Years on Washington Square." *New York Historical Society Quarterly* (July 1948), 154–61.

Klossowski de Rola, Stanislas. *Alchemy: The Secret Art*. London: Thames and Hudson, 1973.

Knox College Catalogues, 1855–1870, Galesburg, IL.

Knox College Reports Presented to the Board of Trustees at their Annual Meeting. June 25, 1856, Galesburg: Knox College, 1856.

Knox Student, Knox College, Galesburg, IL 1924–1938

Knoxiana and *Oak Leaf*, Knox College and Sherman Book Printer, Galesburg, IL, 1856–1857.

Knoxville Journal, 1855–1857. Knoxville, IL.

Koeper, Frederick. *Illinois Architecture from Territorial Times to the Present; A Selective Guide*. Chicago: University of Chicago Press, 1968.

Kowsky,Francis R. "Simplicity and Dignity: The Public and Institutional Buildings of Alexander Jackson Davis," in *Alexander Jackson Davis, American Architect, 1803–1892*, edited by Amelia Peck. New York: Rizzoli and Metropolitan Museum of Art, 1992.

Kutalowski, Katherine. "Anti-Masonry Reexamined." *Journal of American History*. 71 (September 1984), 269–93.

Lawlor, Robert. *Sacred Geometry: Philosophy and Practice*. New York: Crossroad, 1982.

Livio, Mario. *The Golden Ratio: The Story of Phi, the World's Most Astonishing Number*. New York: Broadway Books, 2002.

Lomas, Robert. *The Secrets of Freemasonry: Revealing the Suppressed Tradition*. London: Magpie Books, 2006.

Loth, Calder, and Julius T. Sadler Jr. *The Only Proper Style: Gothic Architecture in America*. Boston: New York Graphic Society, 1975.

MacNulty, W. Kirk. *Freemasonry, A Journey through Ritual and Symbol*. London: Thames and Hudson, 1991.

Mackey, Albert G. *Encyclopedia of Freemasonry and its Kindred Sciences Comprising the Whole Range of Arts, Sciences and Literature as Connected with the Institution*. Philadelphia: McClure Publishers, 1917.

———. *The History of Freemasonry: The Legends of the Craft*. Reprint edition. New York: Barnes and Noble, 1998.

———. *A Lexicon of Freemasonry*. Reprint edition. New York: Barnes and Noble, 2004.

———. *The Point Within A Circle and Its Masonic Significance*. New York: Kessinger Publishing, 2006.

Monmouth Courier, 1867–1868. Monmouth, IL.

Muelder, Hermann R. *Fighters for Freedom: The History of Anti-Slavery Activities of Men and Women Associated with Knox College*. New York: Columbia University Press, 1959.

———. *Missionaries and Muckrakers: The First Hundred Years of Knox College*. Urbana: University of Illinois Press, 1984.

Newman, Rochelle, and Martha Boles. *The Golden Relationship: Art, Math & Nature*. Vol. 1 (Second Edition). Bradford, MA: Pythagorean Press, 1992.

Newton, Roger Hale. *Town and Davis, Architects*. New York: Columbia University Press, 1942.

New York Daily News, 1836–1840.

Nichols, Fredrick D. *Palladio in America*. New York: Rizzoli, 1978.

Norman, Matthew. "From an 'Abolition City' to the Color Line: Galesburg, Knox College, and the Legacy of Antislavery Activism." *Journal of Illinois History*. Spring 2007, 1–26.

Olson, Ernest. *The Swedish Element in Illinois, A Survey of the Past Seven Decades*. Chicago: Swedish-American Biographical Association, 1917.

Olsson, Nils William. *Swedish Passenger Arrivals in New York 1820–1850*. Chicago: Swedish Pioneer Historical Society, 1967.

Palladio, Andrea. *The Four Books of Architecture*. London: 1790. Translated by Isaac Ware. Reprint, New York: Dover Books, 1965.

Patton, Glen. "Chapel in the Sky." *Architectural Review*. March 1969, 172–80.

Peck, Amelia (editor). *Alexander Jackson Davis, American Architect, 1803–1892*. New York: Rizzoli and Metropolitan Museum of Art, 1992.

———. "Alexander Jackson Davis (1803–1892)." *The Metropolitan Museum of Art Presents a Timeline of Art History*. New York: The Metropolitan Museum of Art, 2000. <http://www.metmuseum.org/toah>. Accessed October 2004.

Peoria Daily Spectator, 1855–1857. Peoria, IL.

Peoria Weekly Republican, 1855–1858, Peoria, IL.

Pérez-Gómez, Alberto. *Architecture and the Crisis of Modern Science*. Cambridge, MA: MIT Press, 1983.

Preston, William. *Illustrations of Masonry*. London: Preston, 1795.

Ridley, Jasper. *The Freemasons: A History of the World's Most Powerful Secret Society*. New York: Arcade Publishing, 2001.

Schlesinger, Arthur M. "Biography of A Nation of Joiners." *American Historical Review*. Vol. 50 (October 1944), 1–25.

Scully, Arthur. *James Dakin, Architect: His Career in New York and the South*. Baton Rouge: Louisiana State University Press, 1973.

Shaw, Edward. *The Modern Architect: A Classic Victorian Stylebook and Carpenter's Manual*. Boston: Dayton and Wentworth, 1854. New York: Dover Reprints, 1996.

Sigourney, Lydia. "The Residence and Library of Ithiel Town, Esq." In *The Ladies Companion, a Monthly Magazine*. 1st Series, 10 No.1 (1839), 123–26.

Silk, Gerald. *The Wadsworth Atheneum (Museums Discovered)*. New York: Shorewood Fine Arts, 1988.

Small, Nora Pat. "A Building for the Ages: The History and Architecture of Old Main, (Eastern Illinois University)." <http://www.eid.edu/laclite/coles>. Accessed September 2008.

Smith, John Corson. *History of Freemasonry in Illinois 1804–1829*. Chicago: Rogers and Smith Co., 1903.

Solomon, Alan B. "The Reconstruction of the Ground Zero Area and the Rescue of the Facade of 211 Pearl Street. Unearthing the Esoteric Interests of the Architect Ithiel Town and the Owner William Colgate." In *Masonic and Esoteric Heritage. A New Perspective for Art and Conservation Policies*. Den Haag, Netherlands: Stichting OVN, 2005, 110–19.

Stallworth, Mary Goode. "The Development of Secular Gothic Architecture in the United States." Master's thesis, University of Chicago, 1925.

Stanton, Phoebe B. *The Gothic Revival and American Church Architecture: An Episode in Taste, 1840–1856*. Baltimore: Johns Hopkins University Press, 1968.

Stein, Roger. *John Ruskin and Aesthetic Thought in America, 1840–1900*. Cambridge, MA: Harvard University Press, 1967.

Stuart, James, and Nicholas Revett. *The Antiquities of Athens and Other Monuments of Greece*. 3 vols. London: Charles Tilt, 1792. Reprinted by Elibron Classics, 2005.

Tallmadge, Thomas E. *Architecture in Old Chicago*. Chicago: The University of Chicago Press, 1941.

Tatum, George, and Elisabeth MacDougall. *Prophet With Honor: The Career of Andrew Jackson Downing, 1815–1852*. Washington, D.C: Dumbarton Oaks, 1987.

Taylor, Alice Felt. *Freedom's Ferment: Phases of American Social History to 1860*. New York: Harper and Row, 1944.

Taylor, Richard S. "Seeking the Kingdom: A Study in the Career of Jonathan Blanchard, 1811–1892." Ph.D. diss., Northern Illinois University, Dekalb, IL, December 1977.

Taylor, Thomas. *The Theoretic Arithmetic of the Pythagoreans*. London: Prometheus Press Reprints, 2006.

———. Introduction in *Philosophical and Mathematical Commentaries of Proclus on the First Book of Euclid's Elements*. Translated by Thomas Taylor, London: Prometheus Trust Press Reprints, 2006; reprint of the 1792 Payne and Egerton, London, edition.

———. (trans.) *The Golden Fleece—containing the Mirror of Alchemy*. London: Prometheus Press, 2005.

Temple, Wayne C., and Temple, Sunderine. *Abraham Lincoln and Illinois' Fifth Capitol*. Mahomet, Illinois: Mayhaven, 1988.

Turnbull, Everett R. *The Rise and Progress of Freemasonry in Illinois 1783–1952*. Springfield: Grand Lodge of Illinois, 1952.

Turner, Paul Venable. *Campus: An American Planning Tradition*. New York: Architectural History Foundation; Cambridge, MA: MIT Press, 1984.

United States Census of 1850. Washington, D.C.: 1853.

Vaughn, William Preston. *The Anti-Masonic Party*. Lexington: University of Kentucky Press, 1983.

Versluis, Arthur. *Esoteric Origins of the American Renaissance*. New York: Oxford University Press, 2001.

Vitruvius, Pollio. *The Ten Books of Architecture*. Translated by Morris H. Morgan. Cambridge: Harvard University Press, 1914; New York: Dover Books, 1996.

Waite, A.E. *The Secret Tradition in Freemasonry*. London: 1911. Reprint edition: Kessinger Publishing, 2006.

Ward, J.S.M. *Freemasonry and the Ancient Gods*. London: Simpkin, Marshall, Hamilton, Kent & Co. Ltd., 1921.

Warren, Amos. *The Young Man's Best Companion: Or Mathematical Compendium, Containing a Great Variety of Very Useful Rules and Examples in Mathematics*. Liverpool: Nuttal, Fisher, and Dixon, 1796.

Watkin, David. *Morality and Architecture: The Development of a Theme in Architectural History and Theory from the Gothic Revival to the Modern Movement*. Chicago: University of Chicago Press, 1984.

Whyman, Henry C. *The Hedstroms and the Bethel Ship Saga: Methodist Influence on Swedish Life*. Edwardsville, Illinois: Southern Illinois University Press, 1992.

Wiebenson, Dora. *Sources of Greek Revival Architecture*. University Park: Pennsylvania State University Press, 1969.

Wilmshurst, W.L. *The Meaning of Masonry*. London: William Rider, 1922.

———. *Masonic Initiation*. London: William Rider, 1924.

Wittkower, Rudolph. *Architectural Principles in the Age of Humanism*. New York: Norton, 1962.

Index